Debt Cures® 2

"They" REALLY Don't Want You to Know About

Debt Cures® 2

"They" REALLY Don't Want You to Know About

Kevin Trudeau

Contents

Welcome

Here we go again.

As much as I love writing books, it does kind of bother me to write this one. Why? Because it means the credit card industry and the banks and the federal government are still in bed, still up to no good, still causing us grief.

In a perfect world, we would have been able to move on from this topic and tackled another issue. But the truth is, the situation has gotten worse and I cannot keep quiet. It was not that long ago that I wrote *Debt Cures They Don't Want You to Know About* and launched a monthly newsletter to keep you up to date on all the latest information in the consumer lending industry.

There is just too much new information to put into a newsletter, so we decided a new edition of *Debt Cures* was needed. The newsletter will continue to keep you up to date from here forward.

Thanks for your continued support. Most of you who buy my books know a little about me, but for those who don't, let me introduce myself. My name is Kevin Trudeau and I am a consumer advocate. That means I stick up for you.

Corporate greed is like the attack of Godzilla these days and someone has to stop the destruction. That's the purpose of my books, to inform you and to educate you. Also it is my hope to entertain you while you read as well.

This is serious business that we discuss, but we can have a laugh now and then. And I want you to like what you read so you will remember what you learn and put these tips into practice.

I am not a lawyer or an accountant or a guru. I am just a guy like you who hates what is going on in our country. I love this country and I love the hard working people of this nation and it ruffles my feathers—to say the least—when I see the abuse and injustice that is happening. Especially when the federal government is a player in the game.

This book, as with all my books, is filled with advice, tips, techniques, and methods to help you get out of debt and help you make some cash too. I do have an occasional tirade too, but in general this book is for you to cure your debt.

Times changed since the first book came out and the economy changed in a grave way. New information and new methods propelled this new Edition. We know it can help you.

If you have questions about any topic, see your tax person, your financial person, your attorney person, your voodoo mystic tarot card reader person. I am not an expert. I am not a consultant charging an hourly fee telling you what to do. I'm a guy who writes books and talks a lot on television.

I give you the research and the information that I know can help you. We here at the Debt Cures team believe you need to know what goes on in Washington and in the executive offices of the credit card companies and the banks.

I say it all the time because it is true: Knowledge is power. You need the scoop so you can make your game plan and not be fooled. You have the power to take charge of your charge accounts. You have the power to take charge of your life.

My staff and I love hearing when good things happen as a result of what you read in these books. And while I am on that topic, I need to thank all the people that make this book possible. A book is not a one-man job and I appreciate all the hard work of those who contributed to this project.

Most of all, I thank you, the reader. This information is for you.

Introduction

Let us dare to think, read, speak and write.

~John Adams

You don't have to tell me twice. I am often criticized—in fact, lambasted—for daring to think, read, speak, and write. I can't keep quiet! I won't keep quiet!

I refuse to sit back and take it. I will speak my mind. I will continue to think and read and speak and WRITE! The truth needs to be told.

I honestly think that if more people like me had spoken up, our current economic situation would not be in the awful mess that it is right now. The government types and the corporate executives tried to blow smoke at us for a long time, and they may have fooled some of the people, but not me and not you. And they are not fooling anybody now.

But we all are having to pay.

It's crazy. Who screwed up? They did. Who is stuck with the fallout? We are.

The world, and certainly America, is a different place than it was when I wrote *Debt Cures They Don't Want You to Know About.*

Everything I told you in that book was spot on. And now, the financial economy of our great country has crumbled.

It infuriates me. And I know you are good and mad, too. We should be. They abused us and abused us and abused us, and look where it got them. Crying for a bailout.

I have no sympathy for their whining. I have no sympathy for the banks, the credit card companies, the guys on Wall Street. They made their bed and they are now upset that they have to sleep in it. They can cry me a river and they can take their tears somewhere else, because I don't want to hear it.

They have screamed for a bailout. Consider this book your bailout.

Debt Cures 2 is jam-packed with information that you need to face the uphill climb of today's economy. Times have changed in what really has been a very short time since the first *Debt Cures* came out. I had no idea that we would have to do a follow-up book so soon, but I had no idea the money situation of our country would go to hell in a handbasket.

Debt Cures 2 is your relief package. You, the men and women of America, are the ones who go to work every day, who pay their bills, who raise their children to be decent citizens, and you, the hardworking men and women of America, are the ones left holding the bag.

Do you have a vacation house at the beach? Do you have a private jet? Do you have millions of dollars tucked away? I didn't think so.

Do you have a mortgage or are you maybe facing foreclosure? Do you have credit card bills that seem to get bigger with every passing day? Do you have debt that depresses you? Do you wonder how you are going to make ends meet? Yeah, I hear you. You are the ones needing a bailout.

Let me step up to the plate.

There is so much more going on now that you need to know. There are **new methods** to get out of debt! There are **more magic words** to use to improve your financial situation! There are **more ways to get FREE money**!

Time is of the essence, and never before has factual, trustworthy information been needed like we need it now. They—the feds, the banks, the corporate suits—may have let you down. It's time to face reality and take matters into your own hands. You don't have to be the dummy getting sucker punched. You can fight back and reclaim your dignity and your financial freedom.

Debt Cures 2 is the best present you can give yourself or someone you know who needs a boost and a little jolt of knowledge and power. Investing in yourself is exactly what you need to do right now. Throw off the kid gloves and put on the boxing gloves. Don't let the "big money bullies" push you around anymore. They have pretty much proven that they are all greedy idiots.

> The job at hand is getting your debt cured

If you need something done, who is the best person for the job? That's right. You. The job at hand is getting your debt cured, plain and simple. Times have gotten tougher, no doubt about it. That's why new techniques and new methods are here for you.

No matter how mad I get, I never lose hope. That's another reason all those corporate guys hate me. I don't play into their gloom and doom shtick. I tell it straight. I tell what they are up to and why it is bogus. They are hanging their heads and screaming that the sky is falling, but don't listen to them. Why should they have any credibility now? Puh-lease.

And sometimes all the media talking heads just drive me crazy, too. I want to shove socks in their mouths or tell the whole world to push the mute button on their remote controls.

The sky is not falling. I know that the light at the end of the tunnel is there for you and your debt situation. You have to believe it and see it. You have to go for it. This book is all you need, right here, right now.

CHAPTER 1

Historic Bailout Edition

"Lack of money is no obstacle.
Lack of an idea is an obstacle."

~ Ken Hakuta

Looking at the past, facing the future

You know what? Through it all, this past year or so since the original *Debt Cures* book came out has been absolutely amazing. Amazing in a good way, and I'll get to that in a minute, and, of course, amazing in a not-so-good way.

We have the amazingly crazy things that have been happening in our country, and all around the world, too. The economy has NEVER been like this. What we are going through now is a once-in-a-century kind of crisis. Never in our lifetime—or any time before that—has the nation experienced financial crashes of this nature, like we have been going through lately.

Not even the Great Depression is the same as the mess we have now. That era was a totally different time in a totally different set of circumstances. I am not making light of the Depression. All I am saying is that the events of 2008 are not the same. This turmoil we have dumped on us now could have been avoided.

It could have been avoided!

Sad but true

If ever there have been naysayers against me, people saying that I am full of hot air or just stirring up controversy, I can only shake my head and sigh. Look at what has transpired these past many months. I'd say I hit the nail on the head.

> ...the American citizen is getting crushed.

When I first wrote *Debt Cures They Don't Want You to Know About* in 2007, I pulled no punches. I stated that the bigwig bankers and the credit lenders were greedy and borderline corrupt and that the government looked the other way.

I said in simple black and white typeface for everyone to read that the government regulations are on the side of the corporate powers-that-be, and that the American citizen is getting crushed.

And what happened?

Sad to say, I was right. We are all getting crushed. Stomped on and chewed up and spit out with no regard. Now all those that belong to the Kevin Trudeau "anti-fan club" out there can see that I am not making this stuff up.

Truth is stranger than fiction

The saying goes that truth is stranger than fiction and that is no lie. The lending practices and the basic policies and procedures of how these banks and credit companies do business is beyond belief and now their evil deeds are blatantly backfiring. That should be cause for celebration, but once again, the public is left holding the bag.

It's outrageous! When will it end?!

They have taken advantage of the average consumer for years and their greed has now caused everything to come crashing down—on them and on us. But do they try to do anything to make it better? Do they come to the aid of those they have betrayed? Do they do anything?

NO!

Countless people have lost their homes, a record number of folks have filed for bankruptcy, businesses are closing, and scores of people are losing their jobs. Times are more than tough, and now when people need a little bridge money to help get them over the hump, the banks and the credit card companies are closing their coffers and making it next to impossible to get a loan.

The pendulum has swung completely the other way. If they had applied sound business practices all along, they would not be in this predicament and we would not be stuck in the mud that came sliding down on us in this avalanche of their mistakes.

What makes me angry—angrier than I already am—is that they do not own up to their mistakes. They are like the little kid with the hand caught in the cookie jar and still looking wide-eyed and murmuring, "I didn't do anything."

Not innocent

They are NOT innocent! But who is crying for a handout? The big guys! The rich fat cats are the ones that created this dogpile and they are the ones begging for a bone. "We want a bailout," they whine. Why don't they say, "We screwed up and we screwed a lot of people, and now we want to keep screwing the American public by taking billions of government dollars"?

BILLIONS!

What about the people who are losing their homes—are they getting any of this relief? NO!

What about the folks filing for bankruptcy—are they getting any of this relief? NO!

What about you and me—are we getting any of this relief? NO!

It's all the big boys bellowing for a bailout. The banks, the credit card companies, and now the automakers. Give us money. Give us money. We took all the people's money, now we need the government's money. Even the porn industry has asked for a government bailout because of the downturn in the economy! Gimme a break!

A tanking economy

The economy has tanked, no exaggeration there. The greed and corruption has caught up with those playing with fire, no exaggeration there. And who gets hurt by it all? The average, hard-working American citizen. Absolutely no exaggeration there. The guys and gals who go to work every day, who work hard to raise their children right, and want to make a better future are the ones who suffer the consequences of someone else's dirty dealings.

We the people were trusting and we the people had the American dream ripped out from under us.

But I believe the fight is far from over. I believe the American dream is not dried up. I believe in the spirit of the hard workers of this country and I know we can overcome any obstacle that they throw at us. Their mismanagement (to say the least) does not have to be our downfall forever.

We've only just begun

We can and we will pick ourselves up and move on. The government may not be brokering a bailout for the American people, but I am. This is the *Bailout Edition* of *Debt Cures* and I can't wait for you to apply all the tactics and methods to get back on your feet and move ahead.

A lot has changed since the first *Debt Cures* was printed. The financial world is always going to be a part of all our lives and we need to stay on top of what is going on. When you are informed, you are armed.

So I am back with **more information and new strategies** for you to get out of debt and stay out of debt. For those who have read the first *Debt Cures*, this is not a repeat. A lot of you have benefitted from that book, and it is personally rewarding to me to know that the information I put out to you has helped you to improve your lives.

So many of you bought the first book—thank you—it has now sold to the tune of over a million and a half books! That is tremendous, but you and I both know it's because the information that I revealed needed to be told.

Amazing good

That is the amazing part—the good amazing part—I mentioned in the first paragraph. It has been an amazing opportunity to share with you all the tricks of the trade and expose the secrets of the credit industry. The first book helped so many people and I am excited to be able to continue the education with this bailout edition.

The truth has to be exposed, and the American people absolutely have to be aware of what the United States federal government and the entire credit industry are up to. Are they still in bed together? You bet.

Ripples of change

Have some things changed since the first book came out? Well, yes and no. There have been ripples of change, and perhaps an ounce of credit card reform is in the future, but there still is more to tell and more we can do. And how about the current economy? That mess is certainly more than a ripple of change! We trusted the government and look what happened!

The world operates on the basis of supply and demand. You, the citizens of America, are demanding more answers and more of the truth about what goes on behind the closed doors when the bankers and the corporate bigwigs meet in their luxurious conference rooms. Let me tell you, the furniture in some of these boardrooms is unbelievable.

Talk about sultans and kings, these American fat cats have tables and chairs that cost a fortune. They have ashtrays that cost enough to pay for your kids' college tuition. And yeah, they have ashtrays. We might have a "no smoking" rule in most of our American businesses and public places, but these guys don't play by the same rules. They write their own code of conduct and if they want to light up a big old stogie and put their feet up on a table that costs more than many homes, they go right ahead and do it.

Arrogance

That arrogant disregard is really the underlining of why we are in the situation that we are in. Many children today are diagnosed with ADD—attention deficit disorder. I think the executives who are in control of the financial lifelines of our country have a different syndrome of ADD—arrogant disregard disorder.

I've seen these guys up close and personal. I've sat in on some of their corporate pow wows, where, mainly, they pat themselves on the back and congratulate each other on their methods of making money. You can almost smell the greed in the room.

The smell of greed is not the same as the smell of money. Money's a good thing. We all should like the smell of money; there is nothing greedy or wrong about liking money itself. What is rank is their attitude, the sheer disrespect for anything else than the almighty buck. They choose to pay no attention to anyone or anything but themselves and their bottom line.

> ...nothing evil about making money or wanting money.

I want to be rich

Let me be the first to point out that there is nothing evil about making money or wanting money. It's the American way. It's human nature. I have no qualms telling you that I want to be rich. I will never deny that. I'm an entrepreneur. Making money is what I do. I bet you would say the same thing yourself. "I want to be rich." Go ahead. Say it. "I want to be rich." What I don't hear you saying is that you want to get rich at any cost, no matter how many people, laws, or moral codes you may step on along the way.

That's the difference between the people in power that are making the rules and those who are in the real world struggling from day to day to pay the bills and make ends meet. The hard-working folks in our country know that there is a little something called character and ethics and not taking advantage of the little guy.

There is also a whole other world out there though, the "big boys" of the credit industry, the banking industry, and the lobbyists and the senators who make the laws and regulations. The playbook they carry is their own and they think they are the only ones who get to play by their rules, because they are the ones who are making up their rules.

It is grossly unfair.

Demand the truth

But let's get back to supply and demand. You, the honest worker of this country, are demanding the answers. You demand the truth. That is what I am here to supply. Many of the games that they play were exposed in the first *Debt Cures* book. Due to the success of that book, millions of people have started paying attention to what is going on in Washington and with the credit lending industry, and things are starting to change. That is exciting.

If you take away only one point from everything offered in these pages, I want you to know that you do not have to take their crap. I am here to tell you—don't ever underestimate the power of the "little guy"!

The most important lesson to learn is that knowledge is power and the more you know, the more you can fight back. I am here to give you more. In the first *Debt Cures They Don't Want You to Know About*, I gave loads of information on the industry, their back alley ways, and what you can do to rise up and fight. And fight you have!

I gave you tons of ways to clean up your credit report and get your credit score in good shape, and went over the basics of what the reports and scores are and what they mean. For many of you, taking control of your credit was a first, a whole new concept for you. With secret ways to get out of debt and get on your way to making money, the book was filled with great tips and advice that really work. And now it's time for more.

CHAPTER 2

Debt Cures Success Stories!

"Lack of money is the root of all evil."
~George Bernard Shaw

This second edition picks up where the first *Debt Cures* left off. If you purchased *Debt Cures They Don't Want to You to Know About*, I hope you have read it from cover to cover. That is how I operate. I lay it all out. I tell you stories and give you information to apply to your life right now. It is kind of like a textbook, but not really. I never cared for school books. They seemed dry and boring. I believe information can be put out to you that you really can use, and if there is a good story to go along with it, you will remember it better and be able to apply it easier to your own situation.

Keeping it real

So this book will be chock full of stories and examples. A long time ago, someone told me to "keep it real," and that is what I like to do. A few anecdotes may have to be fictitious to illustrate a point, but most will be real stories from the real world. Readers from all over the country have poured in their heartfelt gratitude and success stories, thanks to the first *Debt Cures* book.

Believe me, I know that these methods work, or else I would not have bothered to write the book in the first place. But I can tell you that until I'm blue in the face. Hearing from real people in the real world with real success stories is the only way to convince the doubting Thomases (and your skeptical friends and neighbors) that the methods I present to you really do work.

None of the solutions presented in the *Debt Cures* methods are hard or complicated. Nobody needs a degree or to go back to night school or to hire a translator to decipher any kind of code. I've always thought secret decoder rings were cool, but they are not needed here. You don't need any special tools or special technology or even a secret handshake. I have the information you need, and I feel that it is my duty and obligation to share it with the world.

Simple steps

Simply follow the steps outlined in the chapters, and you (yes, you) can get out of debt and start making money. Wealth creation is also what I want to talk about some in this second book, too. Creating wealth excites me and there is no better way of getting back at the "bad guys" than making tons of money that you get to keep in your own pocket instead of lining theirs.

There are plenty of debt cure strategies to help you out of your financial hole, and when you can see the horizon, I want you to want it! Go for it! I want you to reach for your dreams and feel confident and powerful that you can make them come true. Knowledge is power and I will arm you with the tools to ease the burden of debt and give you wings to fly toward wealth.

Success

I know it's all possible. I'm a living success story. I have overcome adversity and hard times in my life (my past is certainly no secret). Some people will never get it. They think I am just shooting off my mouth, but guess what? People listen. You know who is listening? The FTC. That's right, the Federal Trade Commission!

The feds want me to shut up. They got wind of *Debt Cures* and don't like what I had to say. They want to sue me! Excuse me, but freedom of speech is alive and well in the United States of America. It is my right to put out books and it is my right to expose what I see is wrong with our country and how our policies work.

We the people

I love this country. That is why I am compelled to share all these things that I want to say. You, my fellow Americans, need to know what goes on behind closed doors, what goes on up on Capitol Hill, and what goes on in the board rooms of the big companies of our wonderful nation.

> ... people like you... are now **living success stories.**

Some of it ain't pretty. Does the FTC know that? Sure. They would just prefer that I keep my mouth shut. I've got the IRS breathing down on me, too. So my stories are just like yours. I know of what I speak. And that is why I do what I do. For your stories.

What matters is that people like you, people just like you who bought the first *Debt Cures* book, are now **living success stories**.

Testimonials

In fact, I could fill an entire book with all the testimonials that I have received over this past year. It would be a very uplifting volume, but the purpose of this follow-up edition is to provide you with the latest information in the credit world and federal regulations, what the industry is up to, how you can fight back and how you can cure your own debt. On top of all that, I want to give you more. More ways to get out of debt!

Let me just share with you a few stories of how the first *Debt Cures* book has changed people's lives. You need to know that these methods and strategies can work for you, too. These letters mention some of the tactics that were discussed in the first book. If you are not familiar with them, don't worry. I will be recapping the methods and giving you an update on the latest information or issues, as well as new advice to help you weave your way through the web of government and industry lies and deceit. Oh, what a tangled web they weave. But with the debt cures strategies here, it's as if we have giant scissors or a lighted torch to bust our way right through the messy webs.

This is just a small sample of all the wonderful news received at the Debt Cures headquarters. And when the information packed in the pages of this edition gets out, I know I will be receiving even more letters.

Lori G. sent in this letter:

Hello! We purchased the Debt Cures *book and love it! We have learned so much about the lending industry and feel our eyes are now "wide open" where previously we didn't have a clue! Thank you so much for this wonderful book—and may God Bless You.*

That is exactly my point! That is why I wrote the book—that is why I write all my books. People need to open their eyes to what is going on all around us. We are naïve and trusting and when we let that happen, they—the fat cats with the power—can get away with stealing our money! Not anymore!

Jocelyn C. of California wrote:

Hi, my name is Jocelyn and I would love to tell my story. I would like to tell someone that you don't have to settle or take any crap from those harassing creditors. It is all over when you buy the book. It will teach you how to clean up and keep your credit. It has so helped me and my family. I can live again!

I love that letter! Did you catch what she said? "I can live again!" That is a powerful statement. When a person feels trapped with mountains of debt and the collectors are calling and harassing, it can be a nightmare. The whole family can get dragged down. So many people do not know that there are ways to defeat the overbearing collection rats. Well, not anymore! There are ways, and we can spread the word. The methods of *Debt Cures*—although safe and legal for you—will seem like rat poison to those pest-like collection agents. If you are experiencing the anxiety and hassles that Jocelyn did, this is the book for you. Real life solutions that can work for you too!

Lalla S. of Texas sent a note:

I purchased your Debt Cures *package last month! Thanks for the great advice on tackling debt problems and creating wealth. (I haven't gotten to the create wealth stage in my own finances yet but I'm working on it). However, I have begun the process of cleaning up old debt. Your book and CD have been invaluable. Thanks again!*

These letters are a celebration of success. Lalla has a great attitude. Some debt problems are literally cured overnight, and with others, it can be a process. The power comes in knowing what to do and how to begin the process. That is the most common complaint that I hear when people tell me about their debt troubles: "Kevin, I am so overwhelmed; I don't even know where to begin."

That is why I give it to you straight. No mumbo-jumbo, no fancy jargon, and no fine print. It's all right here in easy-to-understand English. Step by step, you can take back control of your finances and even more important, you can take back your life.

It is telling that so many people are so excited about what they read in *Debt Cures* that they feel they need to write to me before they even finish the book! My mailbag is overflowing with letters like these:

From Dawnette B.—

Dear Kevin and staff, Hello. First I would like to say I have only gotten through the first few chapters of the book and I am very impressed! There is so much information that is already helping me!

From Jose—

Hello, I just purchased your book and it has the information I have sought for many years. Thank you.

From Alex K.—

I just received my copy of Debt Cures *and love the book. I am only to page 85 and have learned so much.*

Enthusiasm can get you through obstacles and these folks all show enthusiasm! I have every confidence that they are sharing what they learned with everyone they know. I encourage you to do the same. There is power in numbers and the more people who are educated about what is really going on will make it harder for the credit card executives and their buddies in Washington to continue with their deceptive ways. Share the *Debt Cures* information with your family, friends, neighbors, coworkers, and college students (especially college students!).

From Robert G.—

Kevin, I received your book a couple of days ago. I'm almost through; it's great. Unfortunately, I wish I would have known these techniques sooner.

We don't want any more letters like this saying, "Oh, how I wished I would have known earlier!" Too many folks have already been ripped off! I want the whole world to know what the credit and banking industry does so we don't fall prey to their schemes ever again.

From Rhonda R.—

I have heard so many negative things about Kevin and his books. Well, I bought the Debt Cures *book and although I am only on chapter 16, I am finding out things that I did not know before and am glad that I got the book. If Kevin needs someone to help him advocate for his book, he could always email me. I would be happy to assist him with research, advocacy and such, but just like he says in his books, you need to ask.*

Rhonda points out several important things. She is not shy about stating that there is a lot of negative talk about me. I've got a reputation and I don't back down from it. I am the most hated guy in corporate America for a reason—I don't cower to them. I don't play their games and I'm not afraid to blow the lid off what is really going on.

I've been "in the know" for several years, was at the big yacht parties and heard the bragging. I've heard the banking top dogs exclaim that not only are they making outrageous dollars, they are making "**obscene profits**!" And they were proud of it. "Profit" is good and normal and accepted. "Obscene profits" are a whole different matter. I could tell you what I think when I hear those words, but let's stick with how the Encarta dictionary defines "obscene:"

Indecent—offensive to conventional standards of decency

Disgusting—morally offensive, especially through an apparent total disregard for others' rights or natural justice.

Their attitude disgusted me, and everything I learned made me realize that most people simply are not aware of the truth and the reality of the credit card and banking industry practices. I took my offense and put it into words—*Debt Cures They Don't Want You to Know About*. This book was a natural evolution for me, as I have already taken on some powerhouses in the government.

My first major book, *Natural Cures They Don't Want You to Know About*, rocked the pharmaceutical industry and took the country by storm. People need to know the truth! Because I am not afraid to tell it, I catch a lot of heat. But I can take it. And yes, as Rhonda said in her letter, there is a black cloud of negativity when my name is mentioned in certain circles.

> You should be able to keep as much of your money as possible.

No one likes the guy who tries to expose the truth when the truth means money. That is the bottom line. It all comes back to money. The pharmaceutical industry wants your money and the credit lending industry wants your money. And the government is right there with them. So, of course, they all would much prefer that I keep my mouth shut and stop writing these kinds of books. Sorry, I can't do that. It is my humble opinion that you should be able to keep as much of your money as possible.

It is wise to listen to Rhonda. She had heard the rumors and stories about me, and was, understandably, a little skeptical, but she bought the first *Debt Cures* book anyway. And this was her response: *I am finding out things that I did not know before and am glad that I got the book.*

It takes courage and integrity to admit in writing like Rhonda did, that sort of confession, "Hey, I wasn't so sure about you, but instead of listening to all the naysayers, I trusted my own intuition, and I ended up learning something." And she took the time to write me a letter to tell me so.

She goes on: *If Kevin needs someone to help him advocate for his book, he could always email me. I would be happy to assist him with research [and] advocacy.*

That is a vindicating testimonial!

We all need to be advocates. We can start a "Debt Cures revolution" of sorts. We don't need to storm any buildings or take any prisoners, but we can speak up and speak out. We can pay attention to what is happening in our financial world and we can tell everyone everything we have learned.

I want to share with you a few more general letters before we get into the meat of this second book.

From Patricia S.—

Got your book. LOVE your book without even trying any suggestions.

I don't know if Patricia's intent was to make me smile, but she did give me cause for a big grin. I'm glad she loved the book, and I assume she fired off the letter before she had a chance to try out the suggestions. I want people to love the book AND try the suggestions. I want the same for this expanded, updated *Debt Cures* follow-up. Yes, love the book, and please, put the methods into practice!

Because my reputation preceded me, there were people lined up and ready to rip apart *Debt Cures They Don't Want You to Know About*. And they couldn't do it. Critics may want to attack me, but the book holds water. I don't have to make up stuff when the truth is so much more compelling than any fiction could be. The scams of the industry are real and the practical applications for your life are real. This review is from the world of internet blogs where there are folks who wanted to take aim and fire at me. Yet they read the book and realized it was good. Kudos to them.

From "*Debt Cures* Review" blog—

Great Book! It's got all the information you need organized nicely in one place. You can probably spend years trying to weed through tons of good and bad information and never feel confident you're getting

*all the information you need. Kevin Trudeau's book is an easy read
and packed full of information that WILL help you. Trudeau is one
of my heroes for his bravery in exposing different scam industries and
he's doing it again with* Debt Cures. *Thank you, Kevin!*

Thank you, but my hero has always been Underdog and the under-
dogs of our society. I didn't set out to have my life be about "exposing
different scam industries," but that is what has happened. From the
greed and connections and deceit of our country's drug companies
to the weight loss industry to the financial wheeler dealers, whistle
blower is what I am. I make no apologies. Somebody has to expose
the real situation. Might as well be me. I have learned to live with
the negativity and the opposition. The powers-that-be may want to
discredit what I have to say, but I get many more letters *thanking* me
for what I do.

From Vanessa—

*I applaud Kevin Trudeau's fight against the FDA, FTC, and
other healthcare entities, as well as the credit and bank institutes,
[and] for letting the American people know the truth and allowing
US to make informed decisions about our physical and financial
health.*

I could not have said it better myself. We all need to know the
truth so we can make informed decisions about every area of our
life. Our physical health and our financial health are so intertwined.
Financial burdens cause stress and stress is the number one health
plague in our nation. Read any poll in any magazine. If Americans
are asked what they worry about, money is at the top of the list.
Taking care of our financial selves is directly related to taking care of
our physical selves.

If people can get out of the burden of debt, a weight is lifted and
the body experiences it on every level. Learning about your financial
affairs and how to alleviate debt AND create more wealth is a major

factor in your overall quality of life. We all want to live longer, stronger, happier lives. It can start right here.

I have one more story for you to read before we move on.

Dorothy N. of Missouri—

After reading the 1st fifty pages of Debt Cures *I was able to cut our interest rates on our highest 2 credit cards ($19,000 and $8,000) from 29% to 3%—saving us thousands. Thank you Kevin!!!*

Yeah, that's what I'm talking about. Results. Money talks. Money in your hand may actually sing. This is not pie-in-sky. This book of strategies is for you to apply right here, right now. You can save thousands too. I have many more examples that I will share with you from other readers who followed the methods outlined in *Debt Cures*—methods as easy as picking up the phone or spending ten minutes on the internet—and they SAVED THOUSANDS.

You can, too. I anticipate getting a letter from *you* very soon. Feel free to finish the book and actually start applying the practices before you write. Don't get me wrong, I love hearing "It's a great book, Kevin," but I really love the stories of the nuts and bolts ways that folks used a technique from *Debt Cures* and saved money. Like these folks:

- ✔ Robert got his credit card interest rates lowered;
- ✔ Cathy reduced her monthly payments by hundreds of dollars;
- ✔ Jalene had old debt deleted from her credit report in 24 hours!;
- ✔ John saved himself $2,000 before he even finished reading the whole book;
- ✔ Randolph saved $2,500 immediately;
- ✔ Francois got rid of ALL his debt!
- ✔ Sylvia got her interest rates lowered and credit lines increased;

- ✔ Pat improved her credit score over 100 points!;

- ✔ Jim had late fees removed and interest rate lowered;

- ✔ Lolita had her interest rate reduced from 30.10% to 11.66%;

- ✔ Vendel & Glen got their interest rate lowered from 29.75% to 5.75%;

I will tell you all their stories and how they did it, and so much more. Like I said, I could give you testimonials all day; for now I'll wrap it up with one last letter from AP in Texas:

We read the book and used one of the tools in the book and we are now credit card debt free. We are saving over $1,000.00 a month by using this tool. Thank you Kevin for this book. We are not only credit card debt free but we are also stress free!!

That says it all. *Stress free.* Are you stress free? Do you want to be? Who doesn't? If you do not want the government and the credit card companies to make one more cheap dime off of you, read on.

CHAPTER 3

Fed and Cred Loan Sharks and Pickpockets

"We believe the American people can spend their money better than the government can spend it."
~George Bush

What is your response when you read that quote?

DUH!

Hell yeah!

Go to hell!

It is not my intention to bash the presidency, and this particular president is history now anyway. We can discuss his failures and his successes over a cold beer sometime, but that statement attributed to him is true, yet the government does not act that way.

Who can you trust?

The American people can spend their money better than the clowns in Washington can. No one needs to tell us that. Sometimes the bozo brigade in Washington makes it quite difficult for us to do that though. They like to keep their fingers in the pot, their sticky fingers, and take a little for themselves. In some cases, they like to take a lot.

I get email jokes just like you do, but this one is no joke. This ditty against politicians has been making the rounds on the internet, and it grabbed me so I want to include it here. Whoever the original source was, I do not know.

"How many zeros in a billion?"

The next time you hear a politician use the word "billion" in a casual manner, think about whether you want the "politicians" spending YOUR tax money.

A billion is a difficult number to comprehend, but one advertising agency did a good job of putting that figure into some perspective in one of its releases.

A. A billion seconds ago, it was 1959.
B. A billion minutes ago, Jesus was alive.
C. A billion hours ago, our ancestors were living in the Stone Age.
D. A billion days ago, no one walked on the earth.
*E. A **billion dollars** ago, was only 8 hours and 20 minutes, at the rate our government is spending it.*

Think about that. That is a lot of money, at an incredibly fast rate. This particular email goes on to make a keen observation on taxes:

Accounts Receivable Tax
Building Permit Tax
CDL License Tax
Cigarette Tax
Corporate Income Tax
Dog License Tax
Federal Income Tax—Federal Unemployment Tax (FUTA)
Fishing License Tax

Food License Tax
Fuel Permit Tax
Gasoline Tax
Hunting License Tax
Inheritance Tax
Inventory Tax
IRS Interest Charges (tax on top of tax)
IRS Penalties (tax on top of tax)
Liquor Tax
Luxury Tax
Marriage License Tax
Medicare Tax
Property Tax
Real Estate Tax
Service Charge Taxes
Social Security Tax
Road Usage Tax (Truckers)
Sales Taxes
Recreational Vehicle Tax
School Tax
State Income Tax
State Unemployment Tax (SUTA)
Telephone Federal Excise Tax
Telephone Federal Universal Service Fee Tax
Telephone Federal, State and Local Surcharge Tax
Telephone Minimum Usage Surcharge Tax
Telephone Recurring and Non-recurring Charges Tax
Telephone State and Local Tax
Telephone Usage Charge Tax
Utility Tax
Vehicle License Registration Tax
Vehicle Sales Tax
Watercraft Registration Tax
Well Permit Tax
Workers Compensation Tax

Not one of these taxes existed 100 years ago, and our nation was the most prosperous in the world. AND we had absolutely no national debt. AND we had the largest middle class in the world.

So why in the world do we trust them now? It's like a bad movie, only it's real.

Who works hard and who works for whom?

Also at issue is how much of your money you get to spend and how much money they are pilfering out of your pockets. You go to work every day and work long, hard hours to provide for your family. The Congressman, lobbyists, and credit industry executives go to work too, but not every day. They don't work up a sweat unless they are on the golf course or playing tennis. They meet up for swanky lunches and take each other sailing and have cozy little barbeques. While you are worried about paying the mortgage and if you will still have a job next month, they are literally jetting around with the jet set.

Every dollar you make has a purpose before you even get your paycheck. Your take home pay needs to go for groceries, and gas (yikes! We won't tackle that ball of fire just yet), and the house payment, and the utilities, and school expenses, and doctors, and dentists, and shoes for the kids.

And the credit card bills. Yep, you are not alone. Most people have credit card bills. Because how else are you going to pay for it all? Some months are tight and a little something ends up having to get put on the credit card.

How many zeros are in a trillion?

When I wrote the first *Debt Cures* book just a little more than a year ago, our country's consumer debt was 2.4 trillion dollars. Trillion. Credit card debt was $1.5 trillion of that. So don't for a second think that you are the only one needing to use the credit card. I don't know anyone who does not use a credit card. The average person had $8,000 in debt then, and now the figure is over $11,000. I hear from people all the time who carry a balance much more than that on their credit cards.

There is no crime in using your credit card. The real crime comes in when the little balance you have grows and grows and becomes a monster—not because of anything you have done, but because the credit institution is allowed to stick it to you.

Today's loan sharks

We don't live in an era of loan sharks and "guys from the neighborhood" charging usury interest, but it sure seems that way. Usury simply means charging an exorbitant rate of interest, and that is how it was; now it is illegal. The loan sharks could go to prison because they would charge usury interest. Here's how it worked:

Big Joey would give you a loan for $1,000 and then charge you 5% a week. Big Joey and his goons would come by and collect 5% of that $1,000 every week, but you still always owed that original $1,000 loan. So, in reality you'd be paying that money forever. The original loan never gets paid down. It could end up with you paying $100,000 in interest on a $1,000 loan, and never be able to pay the money back. That's usury interest.

Years ago, every state had a cap on what interest rate could be charged legally. In one state, in Massachusetts, it was 21.74 %. If the bank or a credit card company charged you over 21.74% in interest, they could go to jail for usury interest because it meant that, virtually, you could never pay back the loan, ever. You were then an indentured servant. You were basically a slave to that company.

Well, the names have been changed, but in this case, they do not protect the innocent. The lending institutions are now limited on the interest rate that they can charge so they can't get away with usury interest, but they can get away with stealing you blind.

That hated four-letter word: FEES

How do they do it? Fees. These guys are creative and sneaky when it comes to fees because "fees" are the bread and butter of the credit card industry. As long as they don't call the fees "interest," they are able to skirt around the rules. They make up a bunch of other names, but they call it all some kind of "fee;" therefore, it is legal. Late fees. Over the limit fees. Maintenance fees. I swear Jesse James couldn't do it better with a gun.

> Fees are the bread and butter of the credit card industry.

I imagine an old Western movie and a stagecoach robbery, yet the guys doing the stealing are the sheriff and the deputy. In my fantasy movie reel, a wide-eyed little boy looks up at the sheriff after he has stolen all the family's worldly goods, and says, "But sheriff, what you are doing is wrong."

The sheriff replies, "I make the laws in this territory, son. What I do is completely legal. I can show you the law books." Then he rides off with an evil grin.

The United States federal government and the banking and credit industry folks work together in drafting laws and regulations that allow the credit lenders to rip off the American taxpayers.

You pay your taxes every year, and what do you get? You get senators and representatives who make deals with the industry lobbyists instead of working for you. That is just plain wrong.

Modern pickpockets

But do you think they care? They care about one thing, their own profit. To meet these guys, and I have in the past met some very upper echelon individuals, they will smile and they will charm you. They can talk a good tale of sunshine, lollipops, and rainbows, but the happy ending is all theirs. These "gentlemen" are almost like pickpockets who will give a genial slap on the arm and a handshake as they walk away after lifting your wallet from your inner vest pocket.

The next thing you know, you go to pay for your dinner and you realize that you are out of cash and you have no idea how it happened.

Same old same old

That is how I hear stories time and time again. "Kevin, it was just one month. Things were tight and I needed to use the credit card to buy diapers and baby food. We have cut back all we can, but we have to pay the rent and the utilities and gas is so expensive now. My husband has a long commute to his job, but there is nothing closer, and he needs that job. So the baby essentials were put on my credit card. And when it came time to pay the monthly bills the next month, things were still tight. I could not pay the credit card balance off in full and I mailed it in a couple days late. The credit card company charged me a late fee of $39 and they increased my interest rate. I could not believe that they could raise my rate like that."

It's frustrating and downright maddening. I hear stories all the time, and most of the time, the dollars involved are much bigger than this gal's tale, but her simple saga really drives the point home.

Snowball effect

It starts out small. You are in a pinch and you use the credit card. Life gets in the way and you miss a payment or you are late, and the fees start. And the interest rate goes up. What started as a small balance has now grown by leaps and bounds overnight, and when the billing cycle comes around next time (and by the way, the credit card companies can change your billing date at any time, too), you have a hard time paying it off and the debt starts to take on a life of its own. It can grow into something unmanageable and you have not even charged anything more on that account. It is nuts. It's crazy how out of whack the system is.

Take a story like that and imagine the balance due is $1,000. Think how much fees and interest pile up on that. Imagine the balance due is $10,000. When you think of how much the fees and interest magnify that, it is the stuff financial nightmares are made of. The scary part is that when you wake up, the debt is still there and it was not just a dream. The bad guys are real and are getting away with highway robbery. The good news is that you can fight back! Learning what the credit card companies can and cannot do is as simple as reading a book—the book you are holding in your hands.

We can be outraged, and we should be. The tactics of the credit industry are downright offensive. We need to take this intense anger and do something with it. That is the name of the game. Sitting around complaining or whining or throwing things gets you nowhere. Getting "revenge" is the best medicine. How do we do that? Learn their game and beat them at it.

CHAPTER 4

Highway Robbery

"My pistols, however, I always kept by me."

~Jesse James

Think of these debt cures methods as your pistols.

When I first wrote the original *Debt Cures* book, I was spitting mad and frustrated and irritated and wound up. Things have not improved.

I swear what we announced—and denounced—in that first book has come to fruition. And the crap just keeps rolling on down on us. (Pardon my crude tone, but it seems like the feds and credit card guys are still spinning their tall tales.)

It keeps coming

The credit card issuers are beyond belief. The state of our country, and the world, has practically bottomed out, and yet, they still keep sticking it to us.

Rate jacking is the new abuse and they issue no apologies. The stories are all over the place. Average Joe from Average Anywhere who even happens to have good credit gets a surprise from his friendly credit card company. What is this gift? A rate increase with no notice, and no reason.

One story making the rounds is a guy in New York, a hard-working dedicated citizen, a nurse. His rate was 9.5% and then it went up to 16.99%. Just because.

Not because of anything this guy had done. Because the credit card companies wanted to make more money because things are a little tight right now. It smacks of brass knuckles and other dirty deeds.

Dirty deeds

These instant rate hikes are unreasonable to say the least. Highway robbery to put it more eloquently. The scene plays out the same all over the country. Here's a notice stating: Put your hands in the sky. BOOM! Rate increase.

Okay, maybe they don't enact a stick-up and point a gun at you, but the gist is the same. You have been a good citizen, minding your own business, paying on time, not causing any trouble. And along comes the outlaw and robs you blind. Except the outlaw is really in cahoots with the sheriff and you are stuck. The banks and the government are playing like the old Wild West.

Those were lawless days and that is how it feels now.

Not fair

Citigroup is among the card issuers slapping the rate increases. They have a lot of card holders and they also took a government bailout. Tell me what's wrong with this picture! They take the money and run AND they stick it to their card holders for even more money! AND THEY GET AWAY WITH IT.

A $20 billion bailout is not enough for them. Their greed is so unreal, they have to put the squeeze on their customers for more money. CNN tried to get a comment from a spokesperson for Citibank and, of course, they refused.

Instead they issued a wimpy statement: "To continue funding in this difficult credit and funding environment, Citi is repricing a group of customers."

"Repricing"?! How about "putting the screws to"?!

And doesn't your heart just bleed for the poor credit card companies in this "difficult credit and funding environment"? They are the ones getting a bailout and they are the ones who created this difficult environment!

Crazy.

The Citigroup execs don't blink an eye. They maintain that everything is right there in the fine print. Ah, the dreaded fine print. If a cardholder does not want the rate increase, they can opt out, but they must close out their account when their card expires. And ain't life just a bowl of cherries.

> Everything is right there in the fine print. Ah, the dreaded fine print.

The $ connection

Things don't change so quickly in the credit card industry on their side of the fence. They have pals in Washington who make slow or no progress toward credit card regulations. The lobbyists for the banks and the credit card companies like to wine and dine their buddies on Capitol Hill, and the results are what we have today. Fine print. They do what they want and shrug their shoulders with a wink. "Why, we state everything we do. Full disclosure. All right there in the fine print."

The Fine Print is tiny legalese that few can read or understand.

The Chairman of the Senate Banking Committee is Christopher Dodd, the Democrat from Connecticut. He has written some "tough" legislation that has gotten nowhere. Is anyone surprised?

His campaign records from the last election show that $4 million was donated from the financial industry. Yeah. I see how it works.

When CNN asked about that connection, his office did not respond. I see. However, his office did make the point that they have tried repeatedly to pass credit card reform regulations and were met with "stiff opposition from the credit card industry."

This is the part where we roll our eyes.

To read the whole article, if you too want to get spitting mad and frustrated and irritated, go to www.cnn.com/2008/US/12/17/credit.card.rates/index.html.

Deadlines

Here's a riddle for you: When is a due date not really a due date? When it has to do with your credit card.

First item of business is to always pay attention to when your bill is due. They can change that on you just because they want to. If you are used to paying on the 16th, it might get switched to the 14th and they, of course, won't bring this to your attention. The credit card folks are hoping you miss the pay date so they can hit you with a late fee.

They're sneaky that way.

They're sneaky in other ways too. Here's a story of a guy named Greg who paid his credit card bill online. No way it can get lost in the mail, it is nothing but a wire transfer of funds from this account to that account. Seems simple and failsafe.

Wrong.

Greg paid on the due date. The credit card company, Bank of America, said that the payment came through at 4:10 pm and the cutoff was 3:30 pm.

Gimme a break!

Sock it to me

He paid online on the day it was due and they still hit him with a late fee! Excuse me while I go into the next room and bang my head against the brick wall.

It is bad enough to get charged a late fee when you are not late, but this story gets typically tragic. Because of the late payment, his interest rate doubled to 28.99%. Greg was told that the bank would not even consider lowering his rate until he paid on time for six months in a row.

This story was reported on a blog called wallet pop and one of the comments from someone named Beth made me smile: "BANK OF AMERICA IS THE SCUMMIEST BANK IN AMERICA!"

(Source: www.walletpop.com/blog/2008/12/02/paying-a-credit- card-on-the-due-date-dont-wait-until-the-afte/?icid= 200100397x1214667589x1200919508)

Circle the wagons

Have you tired of these highway robbery stories? I've got a million of them. I picture the old stagecoach and a band of bad dudes in bandanas pulling them over. The horses come to a stop and the bad guys wave their pistols and start shooting them into the air:

Fees! Fees! More Fees!

They ride off laughing. But we are the ones stuck in the modern day world with the outlaw bankers and credit lenders who keep being reckless with our credit accounts. It is no laughing matter.

It seems like every day I read that the banks are responding to the troubled economy by putting the gun to the customer.

You want to open a new checking account? That requires a higher balance these days.

You want to use your debit card in a foreign country while you're on vacation? That is going to cost you a higher fee now.

You want to use an ATM that is not part of your bank? That is going to cost you three bucks.

On and on

> We get less from our banks, but we have to pay more.

Citibank used to offer customers free overdraft protection by doing a balance transfer from a savings account or equity line. Now they ding you a fee every time. Many banks are following suit. Common customer courtesies have gone the way of the agreement by a handshake—they do not exist anymore.

A research firm called Bankrate Inc. did a study on all these fees being charged by the banks and their result is no surprise. Drum roll please. The cost of all these fees has hit a record high.

Tell me something we don't already know.

We get less from our banks, but we have to pay more. Need to stop payment on a check? It will cost you more. Want a cashier's check? It will cost you more. How about using your own debit card at your own bank and getting cash from it? It will cost you a fee.

Experts predict that bounced check fees and overdraft fees will be $40 or more by the end of 2009. I think some banks are there already. Ninety percent of bank fee income comes from overdraft and nonsufficient fund charges. Just how much fee income is this? $42 billion. Ouch!

Alternatives

Besides using your mattress or a cookie jar, you can switch your money to credit unions or brokerage accounts. You can get a check-writing account at your mutual fund place and usually with no fees for checks or ATM transactions.

The traditional ways are changing. If you want to avoid highway robbery, get off the main drag and look into other options.

From the horse's mouth

An article in *Business Week* magazine (October 20, 2008; "The Credit Card Blow Up Ahead," Jessica Silver-Greenberg) shared some information that I already knew, but is disturbing to people who hear it for the first time.

The banks and credit card companies used to lure you in and entice you to use their cards to charge, charge, charge. They wanted your monthly payments and your interest and your fees. They didn't want you to pay off your balance. They wanted you in their clutches forever, paying a little and always their prisoner.

One gal who went on record confirms this statement. In the article, former worker Cate Columbo states that she was a call center customer service representative at MBNA, which was bought out by Bank of America in 2005.

She said that her job was to "develop a rapport with credit card customers and encourage them to use more of their available credit." It was all a big game to Cate and her co-workers. She was good at her job and claims that her colleagues would gather around her as she bantered good naturedly on the phone with a customer.

They would chant "sell, sell," as she lured the unsuspecting customers to their doom of never-ending payments.

Now listen to what Cate said:

"I knew they would probably be in debt for the rest of their lives."

Talk about the proverbial smoking gun. Your Honor, I rest my case.

Protect yourself

Regardless of what Jesse James advises, you don't need a pistol to protect yourself. A little common sense and a little book called *Debt Cures* can help you out. And follow these steps, my friends. I do not want you to be in debt for the rest of your lives.

Let's get down to business.

CHAPTER 5

Credit Do's and Don'ts

"As more money flowed through Washington and as Washington's power to regulate our lives grew, opportunities and temptations for graft, influence peddling and cutting corners grew exponentially. Power breeds corruption."

~Steve Forbes

It is outrageous and ridiculous what the lenders and banks and corporations are getting away with, and it is mind blowing that the US government allows them to make their money by screwing the American citizen. Banks and lenders and credit card companies are taking advantage of people every day.

They just don't care

The guys in the suits don't care if you file bankruptcy. They don't care if you lose your house. They don't care that you are in debt up to your eyeballs and are being hounded by collection pit bulls and you can't sleep because you lay awake worrying. Point blank, they just don't care at all about you.

The banks and the credit institutions and the credit card companies and the mortgage companies and all the consumer lending companies, everybody that you owe money to, they don't give a rip about you. They're taking full advantage of the good folks of America every day and in every way, and the federal government lets them do it.

A license to steal

I had a banker tell me once, "We are given a license to steal from the American citizen." A license to steal! Signed, sealed and delivered compliments of Uncle Sam and our United States government. That's why we're having such a credit crisis today—because these banks were handed a free pass to filch from the American public.

And, you and I, my friend, have been taking it pretty much in the shorts ever since.

All the companies that give out loans and all the banks are really taking advantage of the unsuspecting, trusting American taxpayers. They pay folks to lobby Congress and it works. The good old boys either pass laws in favor of the banks and credit companies or they do not pass the laws that stand up for you and me. The government has let these banks and the entire industry go completely out of control.

Ignorance is not bliss

I had a friend who always said, "Ignorance is bliss." I strongly disagree. If you read the first *Debt Cures* book, you may remember that the credit card companies are making record profits. Things are tough all over, but the credit card industry is breathing easy. If you made $30 billion in profits, you would be, too. That bears repeating: PROFITS OF $30 BILLION. I like to give a visual aid with this one:

$30,000,000,000

It seems like those zeroes could go on to infinity. Where does that $30 billion come from? Fees and interest from you. Fees and interest from your mom. Fees and interest from the little old lady at the end of the block.

Are you or your mom or the little old lady at the end of your block living extravagant lifestyles? Are you racking up your charge cards with purchases from the exclusive boutiques in Beverly Hills? Are you having a tough time deciding if you should drive the Porsche or the Jaguar today?

I didn't think so. The industry executives making those ludicrous profits have forgotten what it's like to live in the real world. The $30 billion in credit card profits is coming from you, the hard-working American citizen who uses the credit card to pay for the necessary stuff of life, not the latest designer duds or Hollywood plastic surgeries or trendy vacations.

> The $30 billion in credit card profits is coming from you...

Crunch, crunch, crunch

Credit cards are what get us through the crunch times. And then they—the credit card companies and the lending institutions—come along and kick us when we're down. And the federal government looks the other way.

They're aggressive. They're bullies. They are reckless and greedy. I know your mother always taught you to play nice, but now the time has come that we must kick back. Kick them where it hurts—right in their profits.

The most important strategy in any battle is to know your enemy. I know their tactics. I can tell you and you in turn can tell everyone you know. Then they can tell everyone that they know. When the entire nation learns the tricks of the credit trade, the fat cats won't be able to dupe us anymore or ever again.

But we have got a long uphill climb. Look at all the people who lost their homes this past year in the greatest foreclosure debacle that this country (or the world) has ever seen. Millions of folks lost their American dream, all because they trusted the mortgage lender and the government. What a hard lesson it was, and terribly unfair; I can bet that these folks will never be fooled again.

We're living among land mines

Talk about learning the hard way. It makes me sick. We will get into home mortgages a little later, but the reality is that people have trusted the banks and institutions, and they were taken advantage of. There is no excuse for that kind of treatment in this country. In this century. This is not the Middle Ages. We live in the new millennium and sad to say, the good old days are gone. The days of trusting your bank and your government are history. Now you have to know the score or they will take you to the cleaners.

Speaking of knowing the score, we need to do a review—and update what is new—of what you need to know about credit scores and credit reports. For those of you who read the first *Debt Cures* book, you know we went into great detail on this extremely important topic. For those of you who did not, you might want to order the original *Debt Cures They Don't Want You to Know About*. It's a useful reference tool and a great companion reader for this book.

Credit reports and credit scores are the backbone of the credit lending business, so it is imperative that you know what they are looking at—how they are judging you. They are judging you. They don't play fair. They judge you harshly and extremely critically. There is no such thing in their mind as giving someone the benefit of the doubt. The powers in charge want to find ways to make your credit score and credit report negative and damaging to you so that they can charge you higher interest rates and more fees. That is the very essence of what they do.

They want your credit score to be bad!

Score matters

Now ponder this statement: People with good credit are not what the banks and credit card companies want! It is so totally backwards! Someone with a good credit score who pays back their loans on time should be a banker's dream. But no! The banker and the credit card company president want people who are always a day late and a dollar short. They want the people who can only pay a little bit on their balance, month after month after month. That is their ideal customer. Why?

Interest!

Fees!

Penalties!

Those are the three little words that make the hearts of the consumer lending industry go pitter patter. The good customers, the ones who pay timely and pay off their balance each month, are the ones who get labeled as "deadbeats" by the credit industry. There was a great documentary on PBS a while back that tackled this very issue and reiterates the statement I just wrote.

Secrets and lies

The Secret History of Credit Cards interviewed all kinds of people in the know. This is another reason to pick up the first *Debt Cures* book. I featured some of the great eyebrow-raising information from that show. A Harvard law professor, Elizabeth Warren, stated that nobody else would be able to run a business like the credit card industry is allowed. She pointed out that the credit card contracts are written in such a way that is unheard of in any other type of industry. But hey, the credit boys are pals with the Washington boys and these friends let friends do whatever they want.

Professor Warren used the example of buying a big screen television. The customer signs a contract to pay the $1,200 for the TV, with a normal amount of interest for the privilege of paying over time. However, the credit card companies can end up doubling, tripling, or even quadrupling that amount and they can get away with it! It is crazy.

> ... credit card companies can end up doubling, tripling, or even quadrupling that amount...

No one would ever sign a contract that said: "This TV is worth $1,200, but I will pay you whatever you change your mind to every month and I will keep paying forever." With interest and fees, that is what can happen. It is no joke or made-up story that people have made a single purchase and their balance has grown exponentially. The television is $1,200 and that is the amount that the person should pay.

The credit card and consumer loan industry is unique because they can get away with this unbelievable behavior. Imagine you hire a roofer to fix the leaking roof over your family room, and the roofer charges you $2,000 for the job. You agree and sign the contract to pay $2,000 for the roof. When the job is done, Roofer Randy bills you for $2,000. If you do not pay in full the next month Roofer Randy cannot come back at you and say, "Now the roof costs $4,000. Pay up." That is not how the business world works.

If you were to not pay him, Roofer Randy could take you to court, but he cannot just keep upping the amount that you owe. "Oh, look, another month has passed. Now that roof costs you $6,000."

Separate worlds

The credit card companies exist in their own little world, where they can do anything because they have highly paid lobbyists wining and dining the Congressman in Washington so that the laws and regulations stay in the favor of the credit lending industry. The fat cats have worked hard to create this little empire and they do not like anyone to rock their world. I say, let's rock.

The credit card folks whisper, "But it's in the contract." That may be so. Some of the wording may indicate their nefarious ways, but most of us can't read the contract fine print or understand what we read. Many people call their reading glasses "cheaters;" get out your cheaters and put them on so you can read the tiny print and determine what the real cheaters in the credit lending industry are up to.

There is so much that I want to tell you that I get a little excited and get a little ahead of myself. You know that I am a fast talker and I want to be able to type as fast as I talk, and I want to tell you everything in one big fat chapter, but that won't work.

Before we can get into the nitty gritty tactics of what to do and how to cure that debt, and how to find that FREE MONEY and how to start creating wealth for yourself, how about I give you some advice on what **not** to do. That is just as important as knowing what to do.

What not to do

If you ever read the magazine or online articles on dating tips, they always tell you what NOT to do. Knowing what not to do clears your brain cells of all that extra information and emotion that was percolating up there, and lets you get down to business on what to do. (As for dating, guys, do NOT pick your nose; do NOT pick your teeth; and do NOT pick your toes.)

When it comes to your financial life:

✔ Do NOT pay for credit repair.
✔ Do NOT pay for loan consolidation.
✔ Do NOT file bankruptcy.
✔ Do NOT freak out.
✔ Do NOT date two girls in the same evening.

Okay, you can date however many girls you want, dating tips are not my forte. But that could be a fun next project.

What to do

First off, you need to realize that you can get yourself out of debt and you do not need to pay a service professional to help you. You just made the only investment needed and it's this very book. Hopefully, you also signed up for the monthly *Debt Cures* newsletter.

As you know, the world moves fast, and new information is always coming to light. I stay on top of it all and bring it to you every month via the *Debt Cures* newsletter. I reveal the latest garbage that is happening and the latest good news that you can use. Obviously, I can't put out an updated book every month, but the newsletters are terrific at keeping you aware of the credit card industry and its latest shenanigans.

Back to the business at hand. You do not need to pay a credit repair person to make phone calls for you. YOU can do that. I tell you how. You do not need to pay someone to consolidate your debts and create one payment. YOU can do much better than that. I tell you how to ELIMINATE debt, not just roll it all together. Any of the "fixes" that those kind of agencies do for you, you can do for yourself. Believe it. Simply knowing that you do not have to pay big bucks is a step toward curing debt and creating wealth. The more money you keep in your pocket now, the better off you will be.

I do not mean to be rude or insensitive or flippant when I say do not freak out. My goal is for you to stay calm. Think about what all the information in these pages can do for you to help you get out of debt and make your life better. If you need to freak out, I want it to be the freak out of celebration, not stress. You can do the celebration dance when you realize that your life is not destined to gloom, doom, and debt.

Calm your emotions

I realize emotions loom large when we talk about debt. I know that financial woes create all kinds of other problems—medical issues, anxiety, marriage fights, having a short fuse, etc. I know what being in debt does to a person. That is why I want to reassure you that there is light at the end of the tunnel. By not freaking out, you can put into practice all the debt cure methods and you can move yourself forward, on to financial freedom!

> ... you can put into practice all the debt cure methods and you can move yourself forward, on to financial freedom!

Sweet liberty

Freedom. That is a precious word. The banks and the credit card companies want to keep you in bondage to them. They want you as their monthly slave, shackled to fees, and interest, and penalties. They do not want you to know that you hold the key to your own freedom. You can unlock those shackles and walk away.

The key? It's all right here.

Contrary to what many fine people have been led to believe, bankruptcy is not the solution to all your troubles. There are instances when that is the most feasible option, and if you have already filed bankruptcy, don't despair. (Don't freak out.)

Bankruptcy is not a life sentence. You do not languish forever in financial purgatory. You can move on to financial success. But if you are contemplating bankruptcy and have not filed yet and you think it is the only way out for you, think again.

There is so much you can do. Are you ready?

CHAPTER 6

Credit Scores 101

"There is no substitute for knowledge."
~Eli Broad

Amen to that piece of bumper sticker wisdom. I say it every day: knowledge is power. The more you know, the more you realize that you do not have to take the sucker punches that the credit industry tries to dole out. They will try to blow smoke, they do indeed, but I like to clear the air.

Credit, credit, credit

One of the most common stumbling blocks for people is the whole concept of credit scores and credit reports. When I wrote the first *Debt Cures* book, I quoted a statistic from a 2003 survey that said over 90% of Americans had no idea what their credit score was. Thanks to the million-plus copies sold of my book, that stat has to have changed. Millions more of you now know your credit score and the importance of the credit score and what it means to you.

Your credit score matters because the better the score, the better interest rate you can get. On a $200,000 mortgage, just one percentage point can make a difference of $45,000 in interest! No kidding, one reporter says that improving your credit score can save you a million dollars! During the course of your life, getting a better interest rate and better terms on every transaction all adds up to—ch-ching—possibly a million bucks!

So an update of the credit report and credit score bears a few pages and a million good reasons why you want to pay attention. Do you know your credit score? Have you looked at your credit report? Your creditors are looking at your report, so you better believe that you need to take a gander, too.

Credit Reports 101

In the first book, I spent a lot of time on this topic, so I will give you the condensed version here. It is just as important as ever, but for those of you who have already read the first book, there is no need to belabor all the material previously covered. This will be a refresher and an update. I also give updates in the monthly *Debt Cures* newsletter when new information or action occurs affecting credit reports and credit scores.

We don't exactly live in a Big Brother society where the government watches and records every move we make, but your financial patterns are being monitored. The theory behind the whole credit report concept is one of fairness. In the good old days, the bankers and credit lenders knew their customers and loans were passed out with a signature and a handshake. Maybe a few chickens and a few dozen eggs were bartered, too.

Society grew and the folks in charge of lending out the money no longer knew everyone and a system had to be devised to determine who should get a loan—the credit score was invented to be a barometer for creditworthiness. If each person were judged independently and objectively, any creditor could thus make a determination on any individual.

The credit report is supposed to be just that, objective and fair. Every person's transactions with every creditor are reported and a report is generated. It shows who you pay, how much you pay and when you pay. Every month, your bank, your mortgage company, and your credit card companies send in the data on you. In theory, it sounds like no big deal. It sounds like it is "fair."

The reality is a bit different.

The Big Three

The houses that collect this information are called credit bureaus or credit reporting agencies. There are three of them:

Equifax
P.O. Box 740241
Atlanta, GA 30374
1-800-685-1111
www.equifax.com

TransUnion
P.O. Box 2000
Chester, PA 19022-2000
1-800-916-8800
www.transunion.com

Experian
P.O. Box 2104
Allen, TX 75013
1-888-397-3742
www.experian.com

FICO

Every month, they submit the data to another house, an independent number cranking place, and a credit score is generated. If you have also heard the term FICO score, it is because the database place—a software company—is named Fair Isaacs Corporation and the score was hence dubbed the FICO score.

How they compute the credit score is a secret more closely guarded than Colonel Sander's recipe for Kentucky Fried Chicken. But that is also where the unfairness creeps in. The way they compute the credit score is stacked against us. The "secret formula" is not eleven herbs and spices, but is a bunch of gyrations and calculations geared to produce the lowest number possible, not the highest.

It's a numbers game

The whole thing is rigged. The credit authorities do not want glowing credit scores, they want an excuse to hit you up with bad interest rates and fees for the "privilege" of letting them loan you some money at killer terms. The mathematical engineering done to the reported data is a mystery, yet credit experts have done enough research to teach us some important tips.

> The way they compute the credit score is stacked against us.

All the information that the credit reporting agencies turn in on you every month is basically looking for 88 ways to ding you. Eighty-eight ways to make you look bad. Eighty-eight ways to bring down that score. I have no idea what they all are, but every time you make a late payment, it gets factored in. If you miss a payment altogether one month, big whammy. If you have too many credit cards, that is a black mark against you. Yeah, I know. The system set up for "fairness" is not fair at all.

The credit report and the credit score are what lenders look at when you want a loan. They can mess with your life based upon what the report shows, so you need to take it upon yourself to get your report, your FICO score, and learn how to improve it.

Your To-Do list

The first item on your agenda is to get your credit report from each of the three credit bureaus. Why all three? Because they are slightly different. Not every creditor reports to all three. Yeah, I know it seems sort of stupid, but that is how it works. And you will be amazed to learn that 90% of all credit reports have errors. You need to go over yours with a fine tooth comb to make sure it is an accurate reflection of your credit history and habits. You want the best report/score possible—think of that elusive million dollars that you will be saving in interest.

Request each report separately, or you can use the service at annualcreditreport.com to get all three at once. The form to use is available online at ftc.gov/credit and www.annualcreditreport.com. If you don't have internet access, contact them by mail at Annual Credit Report Request Service, P.O. Box 105281, Atlanta, GA 30348-5281, or call the toll-free number: (877) 322-8228.

Make sure the basic information is really yours. It may seem like a no-brainer, but there is probably somebody out there with your same name. Make sure all the accounts listed on the report are really yours. And with the crazy times of identity theft, it is always wise to keep an eye on your credit report to make sure that there isn't any suspicious activity going on or of accounts that you have no knowledge. Identity theft is an epidemic in this country, affecting millions of innocent people every day. Do everything in your power to keep the criminals at bay. Be smart with your private financial information.

Accuracy is everything

Make sure that your credit report is accurate and report any errors or items that you don't think belong to you. The credit reporting agency has thirty days to respond to your dispute. If they cannot resolve the issue, they must remove that item from the credit report. This can have a huge impact on your credit score.

Before I give you some practical tips on how to jack up the credit score, very briefly, this much we know: credit scores range from 300 to 850. Anything under 550, the credit industry considers awful. The credit score is comprised of five basic elements. The internet is loaded with information about credit scores—because there are a lot of "professional services" out there trying to get you to pay them to help you boost your score. Not necessary.

The guts of the score

I used About.com to give you a simple, nonbiased, not-trying-to-sell-you-anything explanation of what the credit score formula is comprised of:

✔ **35% — Payment History**

Takes into consideration the number of accounts you have; if you have any collections activities or negative public records, like judgments, lawsuits, or bankruptcies; if you have any delinquent accounts: total number of past due items; how long past due; how long since you made a late payment.

✔ **30% — Amounts You Owe**

Takes into the computation how much you owe on your accounts and the types of accounts you have with balances; how much of your credit lines you've used; the amounts you still owe vs. the original balances; the number of zero balance accounts.

✔ **15% — Length of Your Credit History**

This is the total length of time tracked by your credit report; the length of time since your credit accounts were opened; the time that's passed since the last activity. The longer you show good credit history, the better your score.

✔ 10% — Types of Credit Used

This takes into consideration the total number of accounts you have and the types of accounts (credit cards, mortgage, car, etc.). A mixture of accounts usually generates better scores than having a bunch of different credit cards. It is such an irony—they practically throw credit cards at us, yet the credit score goes down if you have too many credit cards.

✔ 10% — New Credit

This is the number of accounts you recently opened; the proportion of new accounts to total accounts; the number of recent credit inquiries; the time that has passed since recent inquiries or newly-opened accounts; if you've re-established a positive credit history after encountering payment problems.

> Increasing the credit score is directly tied to decreasing your interest rates.

Yes, I know

Okay, I saw that yawn you just tried to stifle. I understand. Consider this your crash course in Credit Reports and FICO Scores 101. It may not be very exciting stuff, but knowing what they look at means you now know what to look at.

If you were to be judged based on how many free throws you could make, or how many times you could recite the ABC's in sixty seconds, you would concentrate your efforts on those areas. The same concept applies here. Put your attention where the creditors put theirs.

The credit report gets exciting when you take charge and decide to whip it into shape. Increasing the credit score is directly tied to decreasing your interest rates, which equates to dollar signs. More money for you, less for the greedy creditors.

Payday

In a nutshell, your FICO score is primarily concerned (65%) with your payment history and what you owe. It seems like it should be so easy:

- ✔ Pay your bills.
- ✔ Pay on time.
- ✔ Pay enough on each.

Don't get me going on that last one. The credit card companies might give you a high credit line, but if you use it, you get penalized in the FICO score computation. Another injustice of the world. Our hands may be tied, but knowledge is power. Keep your balances down.

Let's take a short break. Go eat an apple to wake you up—apples are better than caffeine. I have heard that you should give any book you are reading fifty pages and then if the story is not grabbing you, find a different book. This is not fiction and I think the tips and techniques coming up will more than interest you. They can change your life.

CHAPTER 7

30 Days to Improved Credit!

*"Any informed borrower is simply
less vulnerable to fraud and abuse."*

~Alan Greenspan

Fraud and abuse. They go together like peanut butter and jelly; macaroni and cheese; the consumer credit industry and the federal government.

Abuse

It needs to stop. "Informed borrowers" are my goal, and the very reason that I write these books. When a borrower is subject to fraud and abuse from their own mortgage lender, and the feds do nothing but blink, something is seriously out of whack in this country. It is so incredibly improper. No, improper is too nice a word. Let's use unethical. Dishonest. Wicked. Immoral. Illegal. Criminal.

I am sickened by the mortgage crisis that swept our nation recently. Thousands and thousands of innocent people lost their homes, their dreams, because they trusted what the bankers and the mortgage lenders and the federal government told them. It did not seem improper for these folks to trust those so-called authorities at the time. A lot of the mortgages were the result of a government initiative. "Let's let everyone experience the American dream," they boasted.

Too bad for all those people now who have no home of their own. The enticement was too great. "Sure, you can buy a house." "Of course, you can afford that monthly payment." "All your paperwork is fine."

Mortgage mess

The mortgage companies gave out mortgages that just a few short years ago, they would never have taken on. Many of the people had shaky credit scores and the ability to repay was based only on the first year of the mortgage. When the mortgage rates increased, BAM, sorry, Charlie.

> The late payments and the foreclosures turned into an avalanche.

The credit industry game of wanting the customer to pay late so they can charge a late penalty fee got a little out of hand. Late payments become the norm because these borrowers were in completely over their heads. It became an explosive nightmare. These folks were not properly informed because the ones in charge who should have informed them were not doing their jobs.

It all came crashing down. The late payments and the foreclosures turned into an avalanche. The only silver lining I can find in this cloud of misuse of power is that it came back to bite the lenders on the butt. They—applause, applause—lost money. Some credit and mortgage companies went under. It is too bad that happened on the coattails of so many others' misfortunes.

Did you get burned?

A lot of people, vulnerable people, got burned and they are still sifting through the ashes, trying to rebuild their lives. Don't let yourself get caught in their fires of deception. If you ever are shopping for a home loan, know the real situation and run the numbers yourself. You have to know what you can actually afford. Don't let anyone talk you into something because on paper it "looks good."

Whether you need a home mortgage, a car loan, a student loan, a personal loan, a credit card, whatever the credit matter, you need to know how the lenders size you up. All they care about is your credit score, so the first order of business, no matter what your situation, is to get the credit score up as high as you can. You want the ball in your court. Get busy and get your credit reports and your score. Get the actual FICO score, not the score on the reports. The credit bureaus give a ballpark figure, but mortgage companies only look at the real FICO score. It costs a fee, even for the credit agencies, to get the FICO score. You can get yours through www.myfico.com.

Then get down to the heart of the matter, upping that score. Join them in their numbers game. Now is homework time for you. Get out your credit reports and play along at home. Some of these fixes are instant. Some take 30 days. In the big picture of life and how much money a good credit score can save you (a million smackaroos, remember), thirty days is nothing and definitely worth it.

Game on

Get the free copy (copies) of your credit report. Fix any easy errors. Any account that is not yours—have the credit reporting agency remove it. An account that was closed and is showing as active, or vice versa, have them correct it. These quick and easy fixes can make a quick and easy increase in the score. (All you have to do is contact the credit bureau and show your documentation; it's a very painless procedure.)

Review the payment history. If you are getting hit for a late payment and you paid on time, you need to file a dispute. Any kind of error like this, dispute it. You will recall that the majority of your credit score is based on these kind of payment detail items. Send in your documentation with your dispute. You can file the dispute online very quickly and then follow up with your paperwork via snail mail. The credit reporting agency has thirty days to verify your claim and resolve your dispute. If they cannot do so within thirty days, they must remove the questioned item from your credit report. Removal of a negative item has a huge positive impact on the credit score.

File disputes. Here is a helpful hint that I learned from some friends who are real estate experts and all millionaires: File disputes. Add that to your list of Two Magic Words. If you want to get a loan and your credit report/credit score is less than stellar, you can beat the industry players at their own game.

Timing is everything. If you are under the gun to get a loan, filing a dispute means that the questioned items have to be removed (after the 30 day window). Until the credit reporting agency can prove that, in fact, the item must remain on your credit report, the questionable negative items disappear.

Your credit score, when these items are removed, will be amazingly improved! That is the credit score that the lenders will see and use to determine your rate and loan terms. You can get a tremendous boost to your score thanks to your genius and impeccable timing.

Get in the habit of monitoring your credit reports. You can use a credit monitoring service to do this or you can rotate getting your free copy from each credit bureau every few months. Any items that are fishy, question them. Why? Reread the above paragraphs.

Delete. I saved the best for last. The grand finale solution of this section is a word that can scare us or put us over the moon: Delete. If you were to wake up one morning and find that all your computer files were deleted, you would most likely be devastated. If on the other hand, you were to wake up one morning and the collection activity that was reported on your credit report was deleted, you would jump for joy.

This is a huge score booster and another one of those little known "secret" techniques. If there is a collection on your account, call the collection agency and <u>simply ask if they will delete it</u> from your record if you can pay. Instead of showing the collection as "paid," they can delete it from your record!

Half of all collection agencies will do this! Many of them do not require you to pay off the full balance. Pay a chunk of it (get the money however you can; borrow from your little brother if you have to) and get this clunker off your credit report. The benefit to your credit score is worth having to owe your brother a few bucks.

Deleting it means it does not get included in the scoring computation at all. Having it show as paid still means a black mark against you. Yes, I understand that you paid it, and to you and me, that is a good thing, but the computer calculators whirr and grind and spit out the notion that having a collection action is a bad thing. It's one of those 88 bad things that the formula is looking for to penalize you.

Having a collection action does a major wallop to the score. Getting it deleted is like a shot in the arm to the old credit score. It makes an AMAZING difference. If you have a highlighter and are marking up this book, highlight this section. In this case, you want to remember to DELETE it!

Did you know that the folks lending you money are not the only ones who use the credit report as a tool to measure you? Your employer can have access to your credit rating and so can your insurance man when determining your rates. The above mentioned methods and timing of disputes can be a handy device when taking out a new insurance policy or when you are up for review at your job. A glowing credit report and you can shine in all areas of your life.

I love helping folks increase their credit scores. It is very empowering when someone makes a little effort and reaps a big reward. People get excited:

I raised my credit score 100 points!

I did what you said, Kevin, and my credit score went up overnight!

It was so easy! Thank you, Kevin and the Debt Cures team!

I've got more up my sleeve. There are more ways to boost that credit score, some so obvious that you are probably shaking your head wondering why everybody isn't doing these marvelous suggestions.

Pick up the phone. This is the easiest phone call that you will ever make. Call your credit card companies and ask if they will increase your credit limit. They love to hear this. You are not asking anything of them except for the ability to give them more of your money. They do not need to know that you have no intention of spending more with the new credit limit. You want it so you can show that your balances are not using up all your available credit.

Remember how that was a big no-no in the score calculation? The FICO folks want you to have less than 30–35% of your credit line in use. Stupid, stupid, stupid, but that is how it is. The quick, easy, no cost way to do this is to have the credit card companies up your limit.

Spread your balances. Another way to meet the silly requirement of not using all your available credit is to spread around how much you owe among all your cards. Maybe you have a VISA with $4,000 on it and the credit limit is $5,000. You are using 80% of your credit line. I have no problem with that. Some idiot number cruncher in a FICO think tank does. There are some instances when you have to throw the credit dogs a bone and this is one of them. Take the $4,000 that you owe on your VISA and split the balance among your other cards. Most credit cards have balance transfer options. You want just $1,500 on this account. Any account with a $5,000 credit max, you are limited to $1,500 to meet the 30% requirement.

Pay attention to interest rates though. You don't want to move a bulk of debt to a card with a high interest rate if you can't pay it off. Getting hit up with more interest charges defeats your purpose of playing their game.

Pay them off. No, this a not a suggestion to grease anybody's palms with funny money. The "them" that I am talking about is your credit card balances. If at all possible, bring those balances down to the 30% range by paying them down. The less you owe, the less interest you are paying out as well. When you are serious about cleaning up your credit report and credit score, sometimes you have to take drastic measures. Maybe that money you had set aside for a rainy day needs to realize that today it is pouring.

> ... money you had set aside for a rainy day needs to realize that today it is pouring.

Getting your financial self in the best shape possible is the key to brighter days ahead. Getting the balances under control is the battle. You have many ways to conquer. If it means hitting up your little brother again, so be it.

Cut your savings. I am keen on wealth creation, but the old notion of "pay yourself first" has gone the way of your dad's suspenders and Aqua Velva aftershave. If you are carrying credit card debt and need to get those balances under control in order to get the credit score under control, think about your "savings" plan.

I know a guy, George, who has a payroll deduction every two weeks into his savings account. He is proud that $200 of every paycheck goes directly to his savings account. "If I don't see it, I can't touch it," he says. George's automatic savings plan is not a bad idea, and I'm not knocking it, but George also has a large amount of debt hanging over his head. So, is George really saving anything?

He earns 4% on his savings and is paying on credit card balances that have an interest rate of nearly 15%. The interest that George is earning on his savings is not keeping pace with the amount he owes on his debt. When there is debt to be paid down, you have to cut the savings and get the credit debt taken care of.

George may be "old school," but sometimes old school ways are still the best. Some of the most basic strategies of money management cannot be overlooked. If you have credit card debt (and face it, who doesn't it?), and you are working on improving your credit score, start at square one. Take a deep breath, clear your mind, and listen to the simple wisdom of our elders.

Pay your bills on time. Okey dokey. No brain surgery or rocket science there. But let's be honest, do you always pay your bills on time? We are all fallible human beings with jobs, kids, PTA, the mother-in-law coming to visit, the pain-in-the-butt boss, groceries to buy, laundry to do, a school science project due (tomorrow), a birthday gift to buy, and a hundred other things every day that take our attention away from the monotony of paying the bills.

If you have never, ever, made a late payment in the history of your adult life, please raise your hand. I want to personally congratulate you. You are a rarity. The rest of us are mere mortals who have let the VISA bill get buried on the kitchen counter or the hall desk for a week. In the three-step process of writing the check, finding a stamp, and getting the envelope to the mailbox, getting it to the mailbox is my weakness.

Even with the advent of paying bills online, late payments can still happen. I have friends who have it set up that their bills are automatically paid every month, but I only do that for the mortgage payment and the car payment that are the same amount each month. The credit card bill is different each month so I enter it into the bill pay system online through my bank. It's easy to do, but some months, time has gotten away from me and the due dates for bills passed me by and yep, it's another late payment.

I have taken a long time to say, yeah, I know we all, from time to time, forget to pay our bills by the due date. But wow, now that I know how much it affects the credit report and credit score, I will turn over a new leaf. I used to think that a late payment was not a big deal. They got my payment. Life goes on.

The credit people are very unforgiving in how they calculate the FICO score, and it is the truth that little things mean a lot. Little things that we can control, we should control. Mailing your payment timely or setting it up online to be paid on time should now be a priority for every one of us. Late payments are like dollars blowing out of your wallet and into the sky floating up and out of your grasp. When you pay late, you are giving the creditor the right to hit you up with an outrageous late fee, and worse, you set yourself up for the whammy of the bad credit score.

Don't ever miss a payment. If the aforementioned snafus occur, send in your payment, even if it is late. Skipping a payment is bad, bad, really bad. If you miss a payment, they rub their hands together and can increase your interest rate faster than you can say blink. One missed payment and they will use it against you. Skipped payments are a killer for the credit score as well.

If you are going through tough times, ignoring your payments will not make the situation any better. Several missed months and the creditor may feel inclined to turn your account over to collection. Having collection agency activity on your credit report is one of the biggies. It brings your credit score down like a lead balloon. It is one of those lingering items, too. It can hang around, weighing you down for up to seven years.

When the proverbial crap hits the fan in your life, call your creditors and negotiate some kind of payment arrangement. Any payment will reflect better on your credit than hiding under the bed wishing it all would just go away. And it will go away eventually. Hang tight and you will learn the methods to cure your debt and you will never find yourself in this predicament again.

> ...the best thing for your credit score is to have accounts with good payment history

Keep your accounts open. This method always surprises people. "But Kevin," they tell me, "I thought I should close out all my old accounts that I don't use anymore." My reply is sometimes and sometimes not.

One of the ways to get good credit—to jump up that score—is to show that you have a history of good payment. If your old accounts were troublesome and your track record was not so great, go ahead and close them. On the other hand, if you have a credit card account that you no longer use, but it shows that you always paid and always paid on time, then keep it open. A good reflection on your credit history can counteract some of the other negative items. You don't have to use the card or that account anymore. Just let it stay open so the credit score formula includes it in the number crunching.

Credit experts say that the best thing for your credit score is to have accounts with good payment history that are five years running. It shows you are a good credit risk. If you've got it, flaunt it.

Don't have too many credit cards. Every day you are bombarded with credit card offers. Ignore them. One or two cards is all you really need. Department store charge accounts are usually not worth it. They charge notoriously high interest rates and the little bit of savings they give you with the initial offer (usually 10% of your purchases that day) do not warrant opening another credit account.

The credit industry has a double standard. They want you to get all these cards that they mail you every day and hound you with at the mall and sporting events, but the credit score calculation holds it against you if you have too many accounts.

Don't go credit happy. Same with having too many credit cards, having too many loans in general is not considered a plus in the credit score calculation. Even thinking about getting a loan can affect your score. Every time you apply for credit, be it a credit card or a car loan or a personal loan, that creditor requests your credit report to check you out. Every time someone requests your credit report, it is logged into the system as an inquiry.

Too many inquiries are deemed negative. I think this is another stupid example of their stupidity. If you have good credit and want to take out a loan or get a credit card, for whatever reason, who really should give a damn how many people have inquired into your credit. If you have good credit, you have good credit.

But the system is rigged against you and too many inquiries will drag down your credit score. So while you are in fix-it mode, lay low and leave new credit offers alone. Clean up the credit score and make it sparkle. When you have raised your score and are feeling good enough to apply for a new loan, be particular. Don't bounce around and let everyone make an inquiry.

Every inquiry stays on your credit report for two years. (If you were wondering, if you request your own credit score or a credit card company does a preliminary check on your report before sending you a pre-approved credit offer in the mail, those inquiries are called soft inquires and are not counted against you. Score one for the little guy.)

Mission accomplished. All those steps I just recapped are not common knowledge, yet so easy. Power does not have to come in a complicated package. Get familiar with your credit report and don't be intimidated. Your credit score is just a number and if the credit industry wants to make it a numbers game, we can too.

The banks and the mortgage companies and the lending institutions and the credit card companies do not want you to know everything I just told you in this chapter. They want you to stay in the dark like a mushroom so they can keep feeding you manure.

Up, up, up

If you apply these simple little tricks and techniques, your credit score will go up, up, up. That means they will not be able to shackle you with a high interest rate. Better payments for you, shorter life of loan, less interest. It's a win-win-win. And really, we don't care what they lose.

Why the heck you should care about your credit score.

One word—Money.
Two words—Your money.
Three words—Keep your money.

The credit score is the backbone of the consumer credit industry. Know what makes them tick and you are in control. When we get into all the fantastic wealth creation strategies, you are going to be glad to have more money in your coffers.

If you want to give your money away, give it to your favorite charity, don't give it to these clowns and greedy bastards.

Three friends

The best way to illustrate the differences in the impact of the credit score is using an example of three friends who all want to obtain a mortgage loan. They each want a $500,000 mortgage and are buying similar homes in the same town. Or maybe even on the same street. The difference in credit score means different outlay of cash for the same thing. Do you want to be stuck paying more for the exact same thing as your neighbor?

Madonna, Cher, and Elvis all get their credit reports and credit scores and head over to Big Obnoxious Bank to apply for a 30-year fixed mortgage.

Madonna	700
Cher	675
Elvis	620

Madonna is pretty savvy and she has the best credit score of the three. Cher is middle of the road. Elvis, well, he has been less than vigilant about paying attention to credit matters, but he still is semi-okay with a score of 620. I have read that any score under 550 is considered "awful." None of these three are awful. They are just regular folks wanting a home mortgage.

Big Obnoxious Bank takes a look at the credit histories and assigns an interest rate based on the credit score. This is the moment of zen.

Madonna	6.25%
Cher	7.0%
Elvis	7.5%

Elvis takes a look and thinks what's the big deal; what difference does a percentage point make?

First off, compare monthly payments:

Madonna	$3,078
Cher	$3,326
Elvis	$3,496

The King will pay $418 more each month than the Material Girl. Multiply that by twelve months and he has dished out an extra five grand. Even on a $500,000 mortgage balance, $5,000 is nothing to sneeze at. Wealth creators don't blow five thousand greenbacks, if they can avoid it.

Over thirty years of accrued interest, the numbers get bigger. At the end of the life of the loan, the total interest paid is:

Madonna	$608,290
Cher	$697,545
Elvis	$758,586

Yeah, that's a lot of greenbacks. At the end of thirty years, the three neighbors get together for a burn-the-mortgage-papers party. Elvis has paid over $61,000 more to the bank than Cher. He has paid a whopping $150,296 more in interest than Madonna. That could buy a couple really nice Cadillacs.

Taking the simple steps to improve your credit score means THOUSANDS of dollars in your piggy bank and not some banker's yacht.

If you think credit reports and credit scores and these techniques are boring, or that they don't matter, think again. I can see 150,000 reasons why it is important to pump up the credit score.

One more thing: Pay more than the minimum payment. While I'm in my "schoolteacher" mode here, let me give you one more helpful hint. We have focused a lot of attention on the do's and don'ts of credit score insider secrets. This tip is not exactly a credit report item, but more on the lines of don't let the credit card industry stick it to you. But then again, that is the theme that permeates this whole book.

Maybe you had a parent or grandparent who never bought anything on credit. "If you don't have the cash to buy it, you don't need it or you need to wait until you do have the cash." Different generations have different attitudes, but the current and future generations accept credit as a way of life. Many people I know never carry cash. A debit card or a credit card is accepted anywhere these days. That is handy and convenient and also makes it easy to spend. So, one way to cure debt is to avoid the splurges and the impulse purchases.

That said, I want to repeat that I realize most of you are not in debt because of your "reckless spending." The credit card companies want to paint the picture that they are faultless and we, the people, are to blame for the mountains of debt. We are not binge shopping or doing frivolous "retail therapy."

> To escape their clutches, you have to make more than the minimum payment.

The credit card bills grow because of a job situation or a medical issue or a divorce or a death or a move or school or ... you know, life. The credit card bills also grow because of fees, fees, fees, fees, fees, fees, and you know, fees.

To escape their clutches, you have to make more than the minimum payment. If all you send in is the bare minimum, you are putty in their hands. The credit industry guys and dolls salivate over people who only make the lowest payment. They'll have you in their grasp until the twelfth of never.

The required minimum payment is 4% of your total balance. Think that through. You only have to pay 4%, but is that all you *should* pay? What is the interest rate on your account? I bet it is more than 4%. You will never get ahead and pay the thing down if you continue to be a patsy for their ploys.

Don't be a sucker

They are not being "nice" by letting you pay such a low amount; they are laughing all the way to the bank. Well, they are already at the bank, but you know what I mean. They probably have a rubber stamp especially for all those payments that come through: SUCKER.

If a picture paints a thousand words, an example with numbers is worth something, too. George's sister, Georgette, has a balance on her MasterCard of $1,000. She thinks it is just swell to only have to make a payment of $40 ($1,000 x 4%). Georgette is falling right into their greedy trap. Her interest rate is 14.9%, so you do the math. She will get dinged more in interest fees than her monthly payment. How will she ever get ahead? How will she ever pay this $1,000 balance in full? If the credit card companies have their way, she won't. Georgette will keep sending that little check every month and never make any headway or get anywhere close to paying it off.

How do we stop the game? Easy as pie. Make more than the minimum payment. Georgette wised up and wanted to have this account paid off in a year. Instead of making the monthly payment suggested on her billing statement (you don't have to listen to their suggestions), she knew that she could afford to pay $100 every month. If there were no interest, then obviously Georgette would have this debt wiped out in ten months. Even with the interest, by paying $100 each month, she can have this bill gone in a year's time. If she went along with the suggested minimum payment, it would take over two years and at least twice the interest.

How long to pay off?

It has been brought up that credit card companies should put a little something to that effect right under the box that states the minimum. A small line could be inserted: *If you pay the minimum, this current balance would be paid off in xx months.*

Of course, the credit industry refuses to do so. "Oh, that would be too difficult," they whine. Bull crap. Their software could do that computation in a heartbeat. They just don't want to open your eyes to how long you will be in bondage to them. Well, guess what, I do want to open your eyes.

Keep them wide open, please.

CHAPTER 8

Breaking News: Credit Score Formula

"Of course the game is rigged.
Don't let that stop you—if you don't play, you can't win."
~Robert A. Heinlein

This is yet another reason why we felt the need to put out this edition of *Debt Cures*. Not only has the economy tanked, and the mortgage world turned upside down, and things have generally gone nuts, the folks at FICO decided to change how they score you.

As we have discussed, the FICO score is The One that banks and creditors look at when deciding whether to give you a loan or a credit card, and to determine what interest rate they will deem to give you. 75% of all mortgage lenders use the FICO score and 90% of the largest lenders in the country rely on the FICO score.

Power play

The inner complexities of the scoring process are a closely guarded secret, and the exact formula is never disclosed. When you think about it, that in itself is not fair. If you have to take a driving test, you should be told what is expected of you. You need to know how to parallel park and how to park uphill and how to merge onto the highway. Okay, I can do that.

If you have to write a research paper for a class, the professor explains the breakdown of the grading process so you know what to expect and how to prepare and what to provide.

> The folks at Fair Isaac and the credit bureaus want to keep you in the dark.

The folks at Fair Isaac and the credit bureaus want to keep you in the dark. If they tell you what they want, well, my gosh, the credit industry would not be skewed in favor of the creditors perhaps. Just a thought.

Anyway, for whatever reason, the bigwigs decided to dink with the secret formula. It was supposed to take effect in 2008 and they even called the new score process FICO 08. But the big dogs couldn't play nice so its debut was delayed. There was infighting and lawsuits among Fair Isaac and the big three credit reporting agencies (if you recall, they are Experian, TransUnion, and Equifax).

New score

Well, the fall of 2008 came and went with no new FICO scoring in place, but I'm told that the big babies have kissed and made up and FICO 08 is ready to roll. Or could be rolling by the time we hit print.

The point, they say, of the new tweaks to the score process is to better predict who will default. Yeah, and my crystal ball can predict that too. They proclaim that it is better than "classic FICO." All I can think of is how New Coke bombed and Classic Coke still saved the day. But I digress.

What you need to know

I can talk about their foolhardy ways, and yes I know I do, but the point is moot. This is the new deal and this is how it affects you. So sit up and pay attention, and take notes. Class is now in session.

✔ **Credit limits**—Now more than ever, the scoring process puts the screws to you if you are using too much of your available credit. Unfair, yes. But no one ever said Fair Isaac was fair.

Your score can drop several points simply because you are too high on your credit limits. And now the creditors are willy nilly slashing your credit limits. SO BE AWARE!

Do not run up your balances too high on any one account. Do as we said earlier. Play the spread; pay down; do whatever you can to avoid getting dinged by this dirty missile.

✔ **Active accounts**—This really irritates me. You can get points deducted from your FICO score due to few "open and active" accounts. On one hand, they persecute if you have too many inquiries and on the other hand, they cut you for not having many good open accounts.

With the way things are right now, some creditors are closing down accounts so you get penalized through no fault of your own. Try to maintain open, active, and not delinquent accounts. And as stated above, do not run them up to the max of their credit limits.

✔ **Collections**—this one is good news. Yeah, hard to believe, I know. Small collections issues—as in the original debt is under $100—are no longer looked at by the scoring spiders.

The old score would give a negative ding for any kind of collection activity. The small chump change stuff is now off their radar.

✔ **Authorized users**—this is huge. The original plan of FICO 08 was to ignore any authorized user data in determining the credit score. Think how unfair this is for many, many people.

There are countless spouses who are the authorized user on a joint credit card and have no real credit in their own name. Take your own mother for example. Maybe she never worked outside the home. The dad was the breadwinner. Mom ran the household.

For Mommy Dear to get a credit report with no information because she was only the authorized user on Daddy Dear's account would be a blatant injustice. I like how MSN Money explains it:

> *Adding a spouse or child to your credit card as an authorized user has long been a good way to improve that person's credit score, because your good history with the account typically could be imported to the relative's credit file.*
>
> *But in 2007, credit repair companies began abusing this feature by "renting" authorized-user slots from good credit risks and selling them to strangers who wanted to boost their scores. Some of these strangers bought slots on dozens of different people's cards, boosting their scores by tens or even hundreds of points.*
>
> *Lenders pressured Fair Isaac to drop authorized-user information from its calculations. But consumer advocates protested, noting that the change could punish millions of innocent parties, including spouses whose entire credit history depended on authorized-user information.*
>
> *Legal experts also warned that ignoring information regarding spouses on authorized credit lines could be a violation of the Equa5 Credit Opportunity Act.*

Of course, being in violation would be a no-no. FICO will indeed factor in some authorized user account info into the scoring process. How exactly is anyone's guess.

✔ **Inquiries**—The first talk of the FICO 08 made mention that inquiries were going to be less of an impact on the score. The thought process was that applying for credit was not a predictor of default. In the end, nothing really changed, so you still need to be careful about how many inquiries into your account are happening.

(Source: articles.moneycentral.msn.com/Banking/CreditCardSmarts/new-risks-to-credit-scores.aspx?page=2)

The bottom line

In a nutshell, the more things change, the more they stay the same. The big talk of rolling out a new FICO score calculation is just another indicator that they want control and feel it slipping from their grasp.

> So, you gotta play by their silly rules.

Protect your credit score by doing all the things we discussed earlier. The less of your credit lines that you use, the better. Even if you pay every month, running up the balance is bad for your FICO score.

The score does not distinguish between balances you pay off and balances that you carry from month to month. Seems stupid, I agree, but you gotta know what marbles they are playing with.

Know the rules

So, you gotta play by their silly rules. If you use one card for business travel, for example, and run the balance high each month, stop doing that. Use no more than 30% of the available credit limit at all times. The best thing for your score is to use less than 10% of the credit on that card. On all cards.

I know, it is not fair and it does not make sense. We just have to deal with it. Ask for a higher credit limit on the card that you like to use for travel or use several cards so none shows a big balance at any time.

Watch limits

We are now living in a time when credit card companies like to slash the amount of available credit on your account. You need to pay attention and know if this is happening. If they limit your available credit and you have a large balance on that account, do something about it.

Try to get back your original credit limit. Pay down the balance so you are at less than 30%. Transfer part of the balance to another card with more available credit. Now more than ever, the credit score rates you on credit limit.

The golden rule: It is better to have small balances on many cards than a large balance on one card.

Keep accounts open and active

In our initial explanation of credit reports and credit scores, this point was made, but now it must be emphasized in light of the new FICO 08 scoring.

Keep your accounts open. Do NOT close out old accounts if they were in good standing. You get more points for having open accounts in good standing. With the new rules, you get hurt for having a higher proportion of closed accounts.

Your doctor tells you to stay active and I tell you to keep your accounts active. The new scoring method doesn't want a bunch of accounts sitting there. It wants several accounts in use and in good standing.

A good way to maintain this habit is to put a small regular monthly charge on each card and have automatic payments set up. You want to keep it active each month and you want to always remember to pay each month. The trick is active and in good standing.

Revolving

Credit cards are considered revolving accounts. Car loans and mortgages are installment accounts. They have a set fixed payment every month. Your credit score likes to see you have both kinds of accounts.

You don't have to run out and buy a car or a house. You can get a small installment loan, a personal loan, and by making the payments on time every month, you jack up your credit score. This advice applied to the old scoring ways and even more so now. The FICO 08 wants to see you handle both kinds of credit.

And getting a loan can be the way that you pay down those other credit balances too. Keep an open mind. And yes, keep an open and active credit account.

Blah Blah Blah

Maybe you think this credit score stuff is a bunch of horse manure. Frankly, I cannot blame you. But knowing about the credit score and how they use it and how they compute it puts the power in your corner.

We live in a world where credit scores are the ticket, so you want the best ticket you can get. It is my job to help you get there.

There is plenty of information online about credit scores. Every month, in the Debt Cures newsletter I will provide breaking news as it happens and general info on how to play the game to beat them.

It may seem that they hold all the cards, but not really. We know the score and what to do. By applying the techniques in these pages, you can improve your credit score. Seriously, you can change your credit score and you can change your life.

That is what I love with these books. People write in and say, "Kevin, the information you gave me changed my life." Maybe you will be one of those people.

CHAPTER 9

Magic Works

*"Financial education needs to become a part of
our national curriculum and scoring systems so
that it's not just the rich kids that learn about
money…it's all of us."*

~David Bach

Maybe when you were growing up you heard that "the rich get richer." Yeah, sure, but you can get rich, too. And richer. Anyone can get rich. If you don't believe me, start brainwashing yourself. Look at yourself in the mirror and say it out loud: Anyone can get rich. I can get rich.

Education is key

I agree with the quote above that financial education needs to be available to everyone. Maybe the rich kids get a trust fund for their twenty-first birthday, but most of us have to work for our money. Our kids need to learn how to handle their money because it is pretty obvious that the government and the banks and the credit card companies don't want them to know anything.

It would be nice if the schools could teach some basic facts about money and debt and credit cards. Maybe then our college kids would not be such easy targets for the credit card companies. And easy targets they are. The credit card companies prey on the easy marks. They go after the people that are low income or low educated or just plain young. I think of barracudas on the hunt, circling and smelling for blood.

Since our public schools are government funded, money matters will not be high on the priority list for graduation requirements. Therefore, it is up to us to school our children. Call me biased, but I think the *Debt Cures* books should be mandatory reading for every young person before they head off to college. Would you like me to gift wrap them as graduation gifts?

Kids today, no, everyone today needs to understand that the credit industry consists of two parts. One, it's the people that loan you the money, the credit card companies, the banks, the mortgage companies, the payday loan companies. They make money by charging all these outrageous fees. They're going to bury people in debt, and they know that they're not going to collect on everyone.

The evil villains

So, enter stage right, another evil villain. The collection agencies. The credit companies don't care that you are suffocated from debt and can't pay them. They have figured out another way to make money off you—they sell your debt.

Now, we have a whole host of collection agencies willing to buy all these debts. It's a thriving industry, too. Let's say that you owe $20,000 on your credit cards and can't pay it off. In this scenario, I'll play the role of the collection agency and I cut a deal with your creditor. I buy that balance for pennies on the dollar, maybe for a $1,000. So now, I own that debt, $20,000 debt for a $1,000. The creditor just made a grand and I now stand to make $20,000, if I can get you to pay.

So, I am Mr. Evil Collection Agency Owner. I hire my telemarketing guys, my outbound sales crew ... schemers, liars, scoundrels.

These are ruthless individuals who will call you and hound you to death. They're paid on commission and they are the most competitive breed of animal on the planet. These vermin will say anything to make a buck.

Remember that I only paid $1,000 for the pleasure of harassing you. Anything we collect over a $1,000 out of you is pure profit. So if we get $10,000 or $3,000 or $2,000 or $8,000, whatever, we don't care, we are out celebrating our victory at the bar.

Don't be a chump

Okay, I can't stand playing that role. Those collection creeps make my skin crawl. The fact remains though, they don't expect to get the whole twenty grand. They just use their mastery of lies and intimidation skills, and whatever they get out of you is money in their pockets. They call it chump change because they see you as the chump.

> They fall prey to the bullying and the threats, and they send them money. Don't do it!

But are you a chump? No way! The collection agents are paid a huge commission and they're trained to lie. They're trained to deceive you. They're trained to harass you. In many cases, what they're doing is against both federal and/or state laws. But many people in this country don't know that. They fall prey to the bullying and the threats, and they send them money.

Don't do it!

There are several reasons to not send them your hard-earned dough. Enough rhetoric, let's talk turkey. Let me tell you one of my all-time favorite debt cures methods. This technique is so gorgeous that people have actually cried when it worked for them. It may just be the answer to your debt problems, too.

The number one reason to not pay the collection harasser is that YOU MAY NOT OWE THAT DEBT. Why in the world would you want to pay something you don't have any responsibility for?!

For the WOW files

If you love drama, this strategy can dramatically change your life. If you were to become completely debt free, wouldn't you be giddy? I have several letters from folks who were:

✔ Thank you for helping me get rid of ALL my debt!
✔ We are now credit card debt free!
✔ *Debt Cures* was the best cure for me!

This secret—and completely legal—technique to completely wipe out your debt does not need to be a secret! But there is no one out there telling the American public how to protect themselves. The banks and the creditors and the collection agencies, especially those vicious collection agencies, do not want you to know about this method. If ever there was a nugget that they "really don't want you to know about," this is one.

Take it from me, and from all those who have benefitted from this advice, this secret is a gold mine. It does not matter how much your debt was—the dollar amount is not at issue. Maybe you had $2,000 or maybe you had $20,000. Maybe you had even more. How amazing to be rid of it, totally 100% debt free, forever and ever, amen.

Anything's possible. Let me paint a few examples.

Apply it to real life

Carly had racked up some debt in her life. She had the usual bills and was living paycheck to paycheck. Sound familiar? Then Carly was hit with that all-American blow, she was "downsized" from her job. In the months between finding a new job, she had to use her credit cards to buy some of the basics. Food, gas, strong liquor. Kidding on that last one.

Carly got another job and started paying down the balance on her credit cards. It was daunting. The balance never seemed to change. She paid for months, but felt like she was chipping away at an iceberg that could have sunk the *Titanic*. Then Carly's mom got sick and Carly missed some work. She also had to help her mom pay some of her bills. It was one of those merry-go-round rides that no one wants to be on, but we all find ourselves on at one time or another.

Time passed and Carly moved several times and those credit card bills became a part of her past. It happens. Then out of the blue, years later, Carly gets a call from a collection agency. The account she had owed on was ancient history, long written off as uncollectible by the credit card company. The creditor had gotten its tax benefit by writing it off and Carly was shocked to be contacted by a credit hound.

Know your SOL

Carly was a smart lady and had read her *Debt Cures*. She knew about the statute of limitations. Now you will, too. Everyone needs to know about the statute of limitations on debt!

Most people have heard of a statute of limitations in other areas. If you get in a car accident, you have, for example, a three-year statute of limitations to sue the person that hit you. If you do not file a lawsuit within that window of opportunity, you are out of luck. You cannot decide ten years later to make an issue of it. Life goes on and people need to be able to carry on with their lives without a burden of possible court action always hanging over them. (For the record, let me say, I am not in favor of filing lawsuits just because you can.)

The same principle applies to Carly and other people who have debt in their pasts. They, and you, need to be able to carry on with their lives as well, without a burden of possible collection action always hanging over them. A statute of limitations on debt, therefore, exists for that very reason. The creditors have a window of opportunity to pursue collection and when that window is up, they are out of luck.

Let the secret out

However, the creditors and the collection dogs are banking (literally banking) on the hope that you are not aware of this law. I am amazed at how successful they are at keeping this knowledge secret. Maybe it is because there is not a federal law declaring a three-year statute like we have for some other things.

> The IRS is held to a federal statute of limitations, too.

The IRS is held to a federal statute of limitations, too. For example, you filed your 2005 tax return by April 15, 2006. They have three years, until April 15, 2009, to question you or audit you on that return. If something is amiss on that return, after April 16, 2009, they are barred by the statute of limitations from adjusting your taxes.

For the statute of limitations on debt, each state sets the amount of years. In many states, it is just three years. What does this mean in layman's terms? Carly's last activity on her credit card account was in December 2004. If she lives in a state with a three-year statute, by December 2007, that debt, that entire balance, is off limits to the credit card company and the collection agencies. Hallelujah! Tell the world! So many people no longer have debt and they don't know it!

Of course, the players in this power game do not want anyone to know. They want to shake you down and make you pay. They are good at scaring you, but don't let them. You know the real deal, so don't give them the time of day.

Do nothing

Many times the creditor or the collection agency will contact you right before the statute period is about to blow. They want to cash in. Never forget that you are in the driver's seat. You always are—don't ever let them intimidate you into thinking otherwise. This is what you do:

✔ NOTHING.

Let me explain. First things first. You are no pushover. You don't take threats or succumb to sweet talk (the collection agents try all kinds of ways to get to you). You don't take their bull, and no matter how they spread it, it's all bull.

Whenever you get a call from a collection person, do not ever admit to the debt. The possibilities for error on their part are endless and they really don't give a hoot. They could have you mixed up with someone else. They could have the wrong account. Or in many cases, they could be trying to collect on old debt. No matter what, you stay mum. You cannot trust them so absolutely, positively, do not take whatever they tell you as the gospel truth.

Your tactic is to remain calm. That always throws collection scum for a loop. They are used to playing hard ball and don't know what to do when someone does not get flustered. You be brief, and be firm. Here are a couple of magic words that you need to store in your memory bank: Alleged debt.

Magic words

Let's run through a typical collection call:

Collection Creep: Carly Simon, I have record of your debt to ABC Company in the amount of $10,000 and I demand payment of $1,000 immediately. If you do not send payment immediately, I will seize your house, I will seize your car, I will garnish your wages at your job, I will contact your priest and tell him you are a sinner, and I will get you blacklisted from eharmony.com.

(Yes, I'm embellishing here, but you get the drift. The collection creep will say anything to coerce you into thinking you have to send a payment right away. They will usually ask for a payment, not the whole balance. DON'T SEND A DIME! Remember, your part here is to do nothing. If you send in anything at all, it gets your account active again and sets the statute of limitations running again. Don't fall into their trap.)

Carly: I have no knowledge of this alleged debt.

(Never acknowledge the debt. As I said earlier, chances are that it is not your debt. Sometimes I think the collection creeps randomly call numbers from the phone book and make up some story to scare people into believing that they have some debt. Old people fall victim to telephone scams all the time. Maybe the collectors don't rifle through the phone book, but I would not put anything past them.)

Collection Creep: He pours it on. All his intimidation skills come out full force. More threats. More lies. More phony baloney stories of how he will come snatch your firstborn, and the litter of new puppies, and all the presents under your Christmas tree. (He's a mean one, Mr. Grinch.)

Carly: Excuse me, I have no knowledge of this alleged debt. Please send the account information in writing and I will look into my records.

CLICK. Carly hangs up on the collection creep. She knew to never admit to the debt. Don't stay on the line with the collection caller. Don't be chatty with them. You have one line in this scene. If the collector is legit, they must contact you in writing when you request it. Sometimes—oftentimes—they will call repeatedly. Your script never changes: I have no knowledge of this alleged debt. Especially if the statute is looming, do not give them any ammunition to use against you. Wait it out. Silently. Time is on your side.

Use your smarts

Okay, so you have that line down. Now the twist is timing. As the saying goes, timing in life is everything. Carly, smart gal, is aware that in her state, the statute of limitations on debt is three years. She knows the deadline on this debt has passed and there is nothing legally that the collector can do. It does not mean that they will stop calling. The call is a quick one:

Collection Creep: Carly Simon, I have record of your debt to ABC Company in the amount of $10,000 and I demand payment of $1,000 immediately. (He does his song and dance routine. You can make up your own outrageous lies here. It's fun.)

Carly: The statute of limitations has expired. Goodbye.

Carly does not need to say anything more. If the debt is old, collection activity is barred. It's a beautiful thing. DEBT IS ELIMINATED. Gone. Forever. Wow. For Carly, that means ten grand is wiped away. That's a glorious feeling. The amount does not matter; if the time is up, that's that.

This secret needs to be revealed to all of America. Countless people have paid on debts that legally they did not owe. The statute of limitations for each state is included here for you in the Appendix. Know what the statute is for your state so you are armed and ready to take on the collection creeps if they should set their sights on you. Just to give you a heads up, Alabama, Arizona, Arkansas, Delaware, Washington, D.C., Kansas, Louisiana, Maryland, Mississippi, New Hampshire, North Carolina, Oklahoma, South Carolina, Virginia, or Washington state, all have a three-year statute. Imagine, when the statute of limitations applies, your credit card debt is untouchable after just three short years! 100% of your debt totally eliminated.

Scenario slightly different

Now let's back up a step and not even have a collection agency creep in the picture. Let's make the story be that Carly got sued for collection by the credit card company. Some creditors will do this even though the debt is expired. They think you will cave in and pay. They don't expect you to know about timing of statutes. Carly knew and she didn't cave. She went to the judge and sweetly stated, "Your honor, the statute of limitations has expired for this debt."

The judge replied, "Case dismissed."

Ah, two more magic words.

CHAPTER 10

More Magic

"The modern banking system manufactures money out of nothing. The process is perhaps the most astounding piece of sleight-of-hand that was ever invented. Banking was conceived in inequity and born in sin ... But if you want to continue to be slaves of the bankers and pay the cost of your own slavery, then let the bankers continue to create money and control credit."

~ Josiah Charles Stamp

Amen, brother, amen! Let's all gather together and have an old-fashioned revival under the tent canopy. The bankers and the mortgage lenders and the credit industry as a whole are in cahoots with the federal government and it is such a blatant game of smoke and mirrors. Talk about astounding sleight-of-hand. They can steal you blind and you didn't feel a thing or see it coming.

We can practice some magic of our own.

The magic continues

Earlier I mentioned some magic words for you to remember. You didn't realize that there was going to be a pop quiz, did you? I can remind you:

✔ Alleged debt

✔ File disputes

I have another pair of magic words, but first let me set the scene. As we have seen, credit reports make the financial world go round. Sometimes they can make our heads spin, too.

I told this story in the first *Debt Cures* book, and I tell it all the time. It needs to be told. A good friend of mine, Kurt, applied for a credit card and was rejected. He was shocked to be rejected because he had an excellent credit history. Kurt went round and round with the credit card company until he was blue in the face.

He finally was told why he was rejected. Kurt was informed that his application was being declined because the credit report showed a $15,000 balance on an American Express account that had never been paid.

Kurt's initial thought was that there had to be some kind of mistake. He had never, ever, had an American Express account. Never. Kurt made repeated phone calls to tell the credit card company that the debt was not his and never was. He told them that he had never had a American Express card so he could not possibly owe one red cent, let alone $15,000. Guess what he was told yet again? "I'm sorry, sir, but your credit report shows you have an outstanding unpaid balance of $15,000 and we cannot issue you an account with our company."

Now it makes sense why we should take a look at our credit reports from time to time. Mystery items can happen to anyone at any time. If Kurt would have requested his annual freebie, he would have seen this item.

Kurt sent letters explaining that he did not owe the $15,000 to American Express or any other creditor. In reply back to him, he only received polite standard form letters. Kurt spent months trying to resolve this, literally months, and then he had a lawyer friend draft letters as well.

It's not mine

Most of us know that sometimes our letters may go unnoticed, we're just an average Joe, but an attorney's letterhead usually gets someone's attention. Not in this case. Kurt only received more form letters. He truly felt like he was beating his head against a brick wall. How many different ways could he tell them, "It's not mine"?

He was on the phone for the tenth time, or the hundredth, or whatever, with customer service—tired, frustrated, exasperated:

Kurt: I have never had an American Express card, ever, in my life. I do not owe $15,000 to American Express. I do not owe $15,000 to anyone. This debt is not mine! This is some kind of mistake.

> He truly felt like he was beating his head against a brick wall.

Customer Service: Yes, sir. I'm sorry sir.

Kurt, exhaling: Identity theft. It has to be. I must be the victim of identity theft.

Customer Service: Oh my goodness, let me transfer you.

Manager: Hello, sir, we are so sorry for your inconvenience. I will delete that from your record right now. I will issue you a new platinum card today, and for your trouble, I will express mail it, so you should get it immediately.

Two words

Kurt was stunned, but this time happily surprised. He had no idea the power of those words, identity theft. Of course, it had to be identity theft. The light bulb went on over his head. Why didn't he realize it sooner? Identity theft affects MILLIONS of Americans so you can bet it will touch you or someone you know.

The FTC estimates that 10 million people are affected each year. That is insane. But that is our reality so we have to be smart.

Play it safe

There are ways to safeguard your information, but crime is crime and the bad guys are getting better all the time at what they do. Don't fall for the old tricks. The scary part is that the criminals are coming up with new tricks all the time.

Take a few precautions:

✔ Don't give out your private information over the phone unless you have called them yourself and are sure of who you are speaking to.

✔ Never give sensitive info over a cell phone.

✔ Be cautious about using your credit card online. Know the site and know that it is secure.

✔ When doing financial transactions on your computer, do it from your home computer only. Do not do anything on a work computer or a laptop in a public place.

✔ Always shut down the computer when you are done.

✔ Only use your ATM card at your bank or trusted locations.

✔ Use a shredder at home to destroy your sensitive papers.

✔ Use the security software on your computer.

It is flabbergasting to people that someone can be using their credit card number without actually having the real card. In the olden days, if a woman had her purse stolen, she knew right away to cancel her checking account and all her credit cards. Now, no one knows exactly when or how the thief gets the information. These bandits are genius. Too bad they don't use their cleverness for better endeavors. Who knows, they could use their technology skills and revolutionize the world.

We can change our world

Well, maybe we can't change the world, but we can change our world. One credit report at a time; one credit score at a time. There are a lot of magic words and I still have more. So far, we have alleged debt, case dismissed, file disputes, identity theft, and another phrase that I did not call "magic" words, but they sure are—expired debt. Remember the statute of limitations? Eliminating huge chunks of debt is pretty magical to me.

> Well, maybe we can't change the world, but we can change our world.

There are other words that are magic:

✔ Debt free
✔ Stress free
✔ Worry free

Maybe I should rename this volume, *Magic Words They Really Don't Want You to Know About.* And the magic is only just beginning.

CHAPTER 11

Medical Magic Words

"Money for me has only one sound: liberty."
~ Gabrielle Chanel

Ah, the sweet smell of money, and the sweet taste of freedom. Can you smell it? Can you taste it?

It is your money, after all. Never forget that. You need to keep it and sometimes it may seem that you need a little magic to do so. Never fear. The magic words of *Debt Cures* just keep coming.

Medical Bills

The number one cause of bankruptcy is medical bills; did you know that? Medical bills can make you feel like you are buried alive. It is so ironic since the idea of medicine is to make one feel better. Once a person gets out of the hospital, sometimes the real nightmare begins—the nightmare of dealing with the bills.

Medical bill collectors are among the hardnosed, hard-hearted breed. They come from a different planet. Hopefully, by reading this book you can prevent your piled up medical bills from reaching the point of collection activity.

Consider your medical bills a priority because the medical industry certainly does. Do not ignore them. The first thing to do is to go over the bills with a fine-tooth comb. The hospitals and insurance companies quite often make errors on the statements and it is up to you to find them.

Question anything and everything that does not make sense to you. When you do reach an agreement, keep records of all phone calls and maintain notes with dates and names of who you talked to. If you are having trouble making the payments, give them a call right away. As with all debt, you can negotiate medical bills, too.

> Whatever your situation, ask and you usually will receive.

Ask for a better payment arrangement. Maybe you need to make a lesser payment this month, but can pay more next month. Maybe you simply need to lower the amount of the monthly payments. Whatever your situation, ask and you usually will receive. And if you are already to the point of collection, negotiate. If you can pay a certain amount, they may consider the entire outstanding balance paid in full. Apply all the tactics and techniques you have learned up to this point and put them to use! You may be surprised at how willing the other side is to work with you.

More Magic Words

Sometimes. As you know, sometimes they—the insurance people—are just plain jerks. Insurance companies sometimes act like they rule the world. They may try, but you are the ruler of your world. Never forget it. I know a guy who had a situation with his medical bills that drove him nuts, until he fired off these new magic words.

I'll call him Dan. Dan had fought cancer, and now had to fight the insurance folks, and the billing wars began. He went round and round, as we all have had to do at some time or another. He was completely frustrated. Over the course of his hospital stays, his bills mounted up to nearly a million dollars. Ouch.

Dan's issue was roughly $40,000 of costs that the insurance company was not paying. The hospital wanted its money and was putting the squeeze on Dan. Dan kept calling the insurance company. It was like the Bermuda triangle of billings. Sound familiar?

This scenario involved some medication and a hospital stay that the insurance company claimed was not covered. Dan spent hours on the phone with the insurance representative. Then he employed the new magic words: "I am recording this call."

Instantly, the insurance rep changed her tone. Dan told me that she seemed obviously uncomfortable. Well, well, well, what a switch. Dan said it was like a miracle. Suddenly, the paperwork was found. After all the game playing, the insurance representative had the needed paperwork that showed the medication and the hospital stay were approved and proper.

Dan had spent hours trying to straighten out the mess, and suddenly with five magic words all it took was five minutes, the paperwork appeared and the proper address to mail the checks was found. Dan did not have to pay those bills—nearly $40,000!—and now you have another set of magic words for your arsenal: I am recording this call.

If you find yourself in a similar situation, remember those words and report back to me any magic that happens.

Negotiate with Your Doctor

While we are on the subject of medical bills, let's dive a little deeper. What if you get caught with no medical insurance and the unexpected happens? Maybe you get sick or injured and get dumped on with huge medical bills. It can happen—it happens all the time—and it can be scary.

Yes, it can happen to any of us. CNN reported a story of a doctor—yes, a doctor! a plastic surgeon—who was without health insurance when he got hurt. He was in between policies, but at the time of his injury, he did not have medical coverage. (And yes, he caught a lot of crap for being a doctor with no health insurance.)

What did he do? He talked to his doctor. He negotiated his medical bills up front, even before his surgery took place. He even said that anyone can do it; it had nothing to do with him being part of the medical profession. This guy needed surgery on his arm and the operating doctor was going to charge him $4,800. He was able to get the doctor and the clinic to agree to half that cost!

If you do not have health insurance, talk to the doctor! The docs want to get paid and if there is no insurance company involved, they can talk directly with you. You are the one to pay so you are the one they want to work with. Make them work for you. You can work out a payment arrangement even before you have any services rendered.

If you have learned anything from *Debt Cures*, it is that you can ask and you can negotiate! Now more than ever, the other party is willing to work with you. Times are tough and the doctors, like everyone else, just want to get paid. If there is no way you can pay $4,800, for example, tell them up front. Use the CNN story of the doctor as an example. If he can get his surgery bill cut in half, so can you.

You never know unless you ask! That works for all things, in all situations! That is the best advice I can give. To me, it is the one perfect magic word that you must always keep in your mind: ASK!

Health Insurance

Right now, unemployment is at an all-time high so there are many people who are without health benefits. Don't despair if you are one of them. You can still have safe medical care and not go broke in the process. There are places that help you find insurance that is affordable or maybe even free. Go online and look up various resources that help people find healthcare such as Healthcare Advocacy, Patient Advocate Foundation, and Patient Services Incorporated.

If you had medical benefits at your old job, you can continue on with that policy under COBRA. You have the same coverage, but you have to pay the premiums now instead of your employer. All employers have to offer COBRA, but maybe the price of the premiums is too steep, especially since you just lost your job. Statistics show that only about 10% of laid off employees pay the COBRA premiums. Many times it is cheaper to go get your own insurance policy than to pay the COBRA cost.

If you are looking for health insurance, compare policies and prices online at ehealthinsurance.com. If you are self-employed, you know how expensive health coverage can be. Never forget to negotiate. You never know what you can get until you ask.

If you have kids, you need to know about SCHIP, State Children's Health Insurance Program. Your kids need health coverage so look into what your state offers. Besides SCHIP, there are government programs for the entire family. Some states have what is called a high-risk pool. You may qualify for insurance for you and your children. And don't forget Medicaid. All you have to do is Google any of these and you will have information right at your fingertips. I suppose that is another magic word—Google!

Prescription Drugs

One of the biggest expenses of health care is prescription drugs. Drug costs can be outrageous. Many people need insurance coverage just for the drug benefits. Now many drug stores and supermarkets have pharmacies that offer $4 generic drugs. Make sure that your doctor gives the prescription and checks that generics are approved, too. Many states also offer discount drug programs. See what your state has to offer. Most take applications for relief programs at the same time as filing your state tax return. Senior citizens and low income folks most certainly need to look into these programs.

Look into these programs as well:
- ✔ HealthWell Foundation
- ✔ FamilyWize discount drug card
- ✔ Needy Meds
- ✔ Rx Assist
- ✔ Rx Hope
- ✔ Chronic Disease Fund
- ✔ Partnership for Prescription Assistance
- ✔ The Access Project

Organizations and Foundations

There is also financial assistance available from the foundations of various diseases. If you have a certain type of ailment, research to see if there are funds available to offset your medical expenses.

Many organizations do have financial aid:
- ✔ Heart Disease: Heart Support of America
- ✔ Kidney Disease: American Kidney Fund
- ✔ HIV/AIDS: The Access Project
- ✔ Hepatitis: The Access Project
- ✔ Vision Care: EyeCare America and Vision USA
- ✔ Caring Voice Coalition
- ✔ National Organization for Rare Diseases

Free Clinics

Don't be shy about going to a free clinic when you need health care. There are federally funded health care centers in rural areas and urban communities. Your tax dollars fund these clinics, so you need to be aware that they exist. If you are in between jobs and do not have health insurance, you simply pay what you are able to afford. The clinic has a sliding scale and you are charged based upon your income.

These health centers provide:

- ✔ checkups when you're well
- ✔ treatment when you're sick
- ✔ complete care when you're pregnant
- ✔ immunizations and checkups for your children
- ✔ dental care and prescription drugs for your family
- ✔ mental health and substance abuse care if you need it

For more information and how to find a health care clinic, visit *findahealthcenter.hrsa.gov.* Type in your address and click the "Find Health Centers" button to find health centers near you.

Part-Time Benefits

If you are looking for work, don't forget about part-time jobs. These jobs may not be what you are looking for long-term, but in the short-term, many employers provide benefits to part-time employees, including health care. If you need a job to get by, try to find a job with benefits as opposed to no benefits. It only makes sense.

Some of the companies that offer benefits to part-timers include:

- ✔ Starbucks
- ✔ Target
- ✔ Trader Joe's
- ✔ IKEA
- ✔ Circuit City
- ✔ Whole Foods
- ✔ Barnes & Noble
- ✔ Nordstrom's
- ✔ Lowe's
- ✔ Nike
- ✔ Land's End
- ✔ JC Penney

Many hospitals and universities also employ people on a part-time basis and provide benefits like medical insurance.

Beat them

A CNN report from June 2009 suggests ways to beat rising health costs. Guess what they say? NEGOTIATE with your doctor! If you are a cash customer, you can deal. Don't be shy. The good doc wants some money and no hassles. You probably can negotiate a satisfactory deal for both of you.

We always get a second opinion on medical advice, and since you know it is good to comparison shop for items you buy, put two and two together. Compare doctors and their prices just like any other service you use. If the mechanic down the street charges less and you like his work, you use him. If the doctor across town is a better deal, go there.

If you have a health savings account through your employer, use it. If your employer provides some kind of health club deal, do it. If your company offers a quit-smoking program, take it. Smokers can be charged higher insurance premiums so if you want to kick the habit, you'll save money from not buying a pack a day and you'll save in health costs.

You are in control

Don't let medical bills pile up and don't let medical bills get you down. As you now realize, you are in control in this arena too. Well, maybe you can't control if you get sick, but you do not have to have the illness turn into an ongoing financial ordeal.

Use these tactics and your medical bills will become part of your medical history. On to bigger and better things with your life. And on to more magic words.

CHAPTER 12

Credit Card Magic Words

"People who grow rich almost always improve their sex life. More people want to have sex with them. That's just the way human beings work. Money is power. Power is an aphrodisiac. Money did not make me happy. But it definitely improved my sex life."

~Felix Dennis

Do my chosen quotes relate to each chapter? Not necessarily. I am just checking to see if you read them. Can I promise you a better sex life by reading *Debt Cures*? No. But I also would say that it certainly can't hurt!

Everything in life comes down to power. Who has the power? And what do they do with it?

Power struggle

Let me tell you again and again that you have the power. It may not always seem like it. It sure as heck seems like the banks and the credit card companies want to lord their power over us. They will try. They want us to think that we are powerless in their shadow.

But they're wrong.

YOU have the power.

You have to believe it and you have to flaunt your power. Don't play the part of the weakling getting kicked when he's down. Think Charles Atlas, or Popeye, or Clint Eastwood, or whoever you conjure up when you think of a tough guy. You are that tough guy. And ladies, you are that tough gal of your choice.

Strap on that confidence and pick up the phone. What's your beef? Credit card woes can be many.

Were you hit with:
✔ Late payment fee?
✔ Over limit fee?
✔ Annual fee?
✔ Increase in interest rate?
✔ Any other kind of crazy fee?

What's a tough guy/gal to do? Demand that the credit card company take care of it! Yes, I said **demand**.

Be demanding

I have learned more techniques, tools, and tricks since the first book came out and this is one of my favorites. If you ever doubt that you have the power, never doubt again! This Debt Cure came from a reader, Tom.

Tom was haggling with the customer service representative of his credit card company. He had read the first *Debt Cures,* so he knew to pick up the phone and call and ask for removal of fees.

After several minutes of conversation, the CS representative said, "Sir, are you simply asking for the removal of these fees or are you demanding?" Being the astute gentleman, Tom picked up on the subtle nuance and replied that he was demanding.

That's all it took. A simple demand. His late fees and the accompanying interest fees were immediately wiped off his account balance.

Wow!

Talk about powerful magic words! One word! Two syllables! *Demand.* When Tom said "demand," his late fees were waived.

Finesse it

This technique is a little bit of a finesse item. Some credit card companies will respond to you asking for the removal of fees. Ask and you shall receive. However, some may treat your polite but firm asking as something they are supposed to counter.

> When Tom said "demand," his late fees were waived.

You should be able to tell after conversing with the customer service representative for a few minutes which way you think you should proceed.

Credit card companies are always changing their policies, so feel out the person on the other end of the line. It may be obvious how they are treating your query or they may even give you the golden opportunity and ask you point blank if you are demanding.

That gives them an out. The CS rep can then write in their comments or notes something to the effect that "the customer demanded the fees be waived or they would close their account. In order to keep the customer, I waived the late fees."

If you get no assistance from the customer service rep, ask to speak to the supervisor. Or should I say, demand to speak to the supervisor.

4 words and 7 words

The magic words never end. Now you see why we had to do this edition of *Debt Cures*! SO much new to share with you!

I have an associate who uses four magic words in everything she does. No matter what the circumstance, her favorite words are: Would you be willing?

Any question, or demand, can be couched with those first four words. Would you be willing to read *Debt Cures 2*? I thought you would. Think of all the uses these four words have and all the doors they can open for you. Would you be willing to …

✔ Remove those fees?
✔ Lower my interest rate?
✔ Give me another month to pay?
✔ Delete that from my account?
✔ Consider taking a lower payment?

The possibilities are endless. Countless negotiations can begin with these four words. I have another colleague who likes the lucky seven sentence. He claims that these words have saved him thousands of dollars every year.

Seven is known to be a lucky number. I don't dispute that. And I don't dispute any of the magic words we offer here. They really work! This particular seven-word sentence is: Is that the best you can do?

If you are negotiating a better interest rate on your credit card, simply ask, Is that the best you can do? If you are buying a car or booking a hotel room, simply ask, Is that the best you can do? This one sentence cuts through the haggle and hassle and gets down the bottom line. You want to get the best deal every time. So ask for it. And sometimes, demand it.

Let's review

We've come a long way from the very first draft of *Debt Cures They Don't Want You to Know About.* My first knowledge of magic words to make things happen in the credit card industry were identity theft.

Now the list of magic words has grown. So many readers have sent thank you letters based on magic words alone. The cost of the book was paid back in spades just by learning a new phrase. People have saved thousands of dollars in debt by knowing the right words to say at the right time.

- ✔ Identity Theft
- ✔ Statute of Limitations
- ✔ Alleged Debt
- ✔ I am recording this call
- ✔ Demand
- ✔ Would you be willing?
- ✔ Is that the best you can do?
- ✔ I have naked pictures of you with the senator

Just kidding on the last one. But I bet it could get some results.

The banks and the feds and the credit card companies keep playing the shell game and trying to make up new rules as they go along. And actually, they are making up their own rules. They can change the interest rate on your card at any time, for any reason, or in reality, for no reason at all. And they do.

But you are equipped with magic words and x-ray vision. You have knowledge, which equals power. **You** have the power. Let's ride the *power* and move on to more new techniques to apply in these ever rapidly changing times.

It works

I get tons of tremendous feedback from folks who read my books. Probably the number one thing that garnered the largest response from the first *Debt Cures* book was how easy these methods really are. And that they work.

> Dramatic reductions in interest rates. All because you picked up the phone.

People don't believe until they try it. And then they are amazed at the results and sometimes feel like kicking themselves for waiting so long to try these techniques. I'm not kidding—these methods work!

The favorite is the simple phone trick. Nothing up my sleeve. Nothing in my hat. Just a telephone is all I need to make debt disappear. The people who try it love it. I get comments all the time, everywhere I go.

"Kevin, it worked! I called my credit card company and they lowered my rate! Thank you!"

I love the thanks. I love that you are applying these tactics and getting money in your pocket instead of theirs. The cards and letters and emails keep pouring in. Dramatic reductions in interest rates. All because you picked up the phone. Maybe you asked. Maybe you demanded. It does not matter to me. You did it and it worked.

Numbers don't lie

Some of the results:

- ✔ 31% down to 10%
- ✔ 15% down to 1%
- ✔ 28% down to 4.5%
- ✔ 30% down to 11%
- ✔ 22% down to 6.5%

Real people, real results. How about that one person who negotiated the interest rate down to 1%?! I love it!

Talk about wiping out debt! Poof, hundreds of thousands of dollars eliminated. That is a beautiful thing.

And dare I say it? It is easy. That little word "easy" causes controversy, but I stand by it. It does not take a special skill to make your debt disappear. Pick up the phone and give it a try. The FTC may want to caution me for telling you that these methods are easy. I will let you be the judge.

I have about a million happy customers from the first *Debt Cures* book who will vouch that some of these methods can be indeed deemed easy.

Cleaning up your credit score? Much of that is easy. Your points can go up significantly with an easy review of your credit reports. Improving your credit score improves your life. It really does.

You get a better interest rate so your payments are lower and you pay off your loan quicker. It makes sense, nothing out of left field there. Much of what I say is common sense that makes cents. I tell it like it is and I encourage you to take what is yours.

Your dignity, your freedom, and your peace of mind. Those things mean a lot. When you get control of your debt, those things feel within your reach again. Getting your life back is the ultimate reward of all of these debt cures.

Try and you will succeed

It is a powerful testament when someone buys my book and then calls up and orders another for a friend or family member because they believe in it that much. If something works, of course, we want to share it with those we care about.

I want to share what I know with you and I am glad to be able to do so. Part of the fun is helping you get out of debt and part of the fun is helping you make some fast money. If you were wondering if we would get to the part of making nice bucks in a nice timeframe, you're there.

Read on. And enjoy.

CHAPTER 13

$10K Right Away

"Wealth is power. With wealth many things are possible."
~George Clason

True statement. I also know that knowledge is power and with knowledge, ALL things are possible. Do you have the feeling of possibilities or do you have the feeling that "life sucks"? Quit listening to the media telling you how bad it is out there. It is bad out there, no doubt about it. And it's not our fault! The blame is clearly fixed on the feds, and the bankers, and the big corporate babies crying for their bonuses.

They got us into this mess, but we are not going to go down with their sinking ship. They dealt us a hand of crap, but I, as always, have a few cards of my own up my sleeve and want to share them with you.

I told you this was the bailout edition, and I have tons of new ways to counteract the miserable financial situation that we are currently faced with right now. So let's keep moving, onward and upward.

Need money fast?

Now more than ever, people need ways to come up with some cash and come up with it quickly. Are you in a jam? Need some immediate relief to a pressing problem or money issue? Just want some extra cash?

Whatever your situation, I don't know anybody who doesn't want to make some extra bucks and do it easily and get practically immediate results. Even if you are not in debt, extra money is a worthwhile venture.

I have ten ways to $10K that I can rattle off just off the top of my head. I bet if you start to think on it, you can come up with another ten ways. Ask your friends. I bet they can come up with another ten ways to make money without really lifting a finger. Well, maybe a finger, but no heavy lifting involved. No time consuming start-ups and no inventory to stock and no monetary investments.

Make more money with what you already have, your brains and your stuff. And did I mention you can do it in 24 hours or less?

Ten ways to $10K in a day

✔ **eBay.** eBay is the way, baby! One way, anyway. I don't get any kickbacks or love money or anything for talking about eBay. It is simply hands-down an easy and sure-fire quick way to put some greenback in your wallet.

I could write a book on how to use eBay, but I imagine there are already books out there that serve that purpose. eBay is hugely popular because it works. You've got something to sell and there is somebody out there that wants to buy it.

Take a look around your house. Go through the garage. Spend an hour in the attic. What has been sitting in your basement for years that you forgot you even had? If you are a "normal" American, you hang on to stuff for the eternal "just in case I might need it someday." We end up with a lot of stuff that we never use. I know a guy who keeps everything, but then when he does need it, he can't find it. So he goes out and buys another one. He has two sets of painting supplies, two of a lot of tools, you get the idea.

Even if you are not a stockpiler or hoarder or an unorganized "where did I put that?" kind of person like my friend, I can pretty much guarantee that you have stuff you can get rid of. We all do. If you can see that your stuff really is cash in your pocket, it makes it easier to part with.

Got golf clubs that you haven't used in three years? Get rid of them. Maybe a bike or roller blades? If you have kids, you have a never-ending turnover of stuff that you can get rid of when they out-grow it or tire of it. Famous brand children's clothing makes a killing on eBay. Their toys, your toys, your tools, the possibilities are endless.

> If you can see that your stuff really is cash in your pocket, it makes it easier to part with.

The beauty of eBay is how easy it is and how easy it is for you to get paid. Set up a PayPal account (it's quick and easy and requires no technical savvy), and the payments you receive are deposited right into your PayPal account. You don't have to deal with credit cards or worrying if the buyer's check is going to bounce. You just sit back and watch the balance in your account go up, up, up.

You could make $10K in a day just from eBay. But there are nine more ways to make fast money. Actually there are many more, but 10 ways to $10K in a day has such a great ring to it.

✔ **Assignment of contract.** Want to make a large sum of cash in an amazingly short amount of time? And want to do so with no risk? I thought you might be interested. Well, there is a slight risk involved. One dollar. Willing to lose a buck? The opportunity to make huge dollars is worth that dollar investment!

An ideal way to turn a quick deal and make thousands of dollars, this strategy is certainly one of my favorites. An assignment of a contract is the key to untold cash in **your** coffers. The possibilities are endless and the sky is the limit when it comes to how much you can make.

Maybe you see yourself as the middleman in this scenario. I see it as the moneyman. Or woman, of course. Basically, an assignment of contract is a transaction between a person who has something to sell and you, except that you do not want the asset that the person is selling. You want money.

So you make a deal with the seller. You agree to enter into a contract to purchase the thing that he is selling. You put up $1.00 in order to make the contract legally binding and you agree to buy the asset for a certain price in a certain period of time, and—here is the important part—you have an assignment clause in the contract. That means you can assign to someone else your right to buy this asset. You don't want it, whatever the "it" is; you want to make some cash on the deal. Basically, you tie up the asset for one dollar, and have the "option" to pay the balance at a given time in the future (e.g., within 30, 60, or 90 days).

You have a buyer who wants the asset, or you find one. You assign the contract to this person for a price greater than your contract with the seller and you keep the difference. Snap your fingers and cash appears.

How about an example:

Bob has a house that has a value of $100,000 that he needs to sell. You contract with Bob for $1 that you will buy the house for $60,000 and your agreement states that you can assign the contract to someone else. You agree that you (or your assignee) will buy the house within 60 days or you forfeit your dollar. You then assign the contract to a buyer that you found who is willing to buy the house for $90,000. You get to keep the difference. $30,000! That is a nice return on a one-dollar investment!

Someone recently did this exact method and made over $18,000. The person tied up a piece of real estate in Phoenix and quickly advertised it in San Francisco. He was able to assign his contract to purchase the Phoenix property to someone who responded to the advertisement and he pocketed that $18,000 plus, with zero risk!

This method can be done with real estate, cars, jewelry, furniture, artwork, etc., etc., etc. The possibilities are endless!! Just tie it up for $1 and assign that asset away!

✔ **Sell your car.** You can use eBay or craigslist or any other online site. You can set it in front of your house with a For Sale sign. You can run an ad in your local paper. You can take it to a used car lot and see what they will give you. You can simply tell a friend to tell everyone he knows that you have a car for sale.

Word of mouth is often the best way to get things done and costs you nothing. If you live in a metropolitan area with good public transportation, you honestly do not need a car. I know of a gal who lives in Chicago about a block from the train station. She walks to everything in her local neighborhood and when she needs a car, there is a car rental place just a few blocks away. She can walk there and rent a car for only as long as she needs, even just for an afternoon.

The money she spends to rent a car on occasion is much less than the cost of car payments, insurance, and maintenance. And parking. If you have lived in a city, you know what a hassle parking can be.

Maybe you simply can't live without your car. Or you think you can't anyway. I suggest letting the idea gel for a while. Motor scooters are a great alternative transportation. And when you need to take a long road trip, borrow a buddy's wheels. Or call the rental guys.

> If you are knowledgeable, you can buy and sell and make a nice sum.

If you have a boat, you can sell it and have a large chunk of change immediately. Are you an avid boater? If not, think about how much you spend on the watercraft and how much enjoyment you get out of it. If you are in a climate where you only have three months of boating weather and you are paying for storage the other nine months, selling your boat can be instant cure and instant fast cash. Again, you can use all the ways mentioned above to sell it that don't cost you one red cent and the net gain can be tremendous.

✔ **Sell your collections.** Most folks have something that they have been hanging on to for years and then they reach a point in their lives when their interests change, and those collections no longer mean anything to them. Are you a collector? Then there is cash to be had.

The baseball cards you have been collecting since you were a kid have value. If the sentimental value is no longer there for you, it's time to cash in. There are other collectors out there that want your stash, and there are buyers simply because there is money there. If you are knowledgeable, you can buy and sell and make a nice sum. You can sell off or you can be a trader.

I know of a guy who is a collector of old and rare coins. He makes great money selling to stores and other collectors. There are all kinds of collectibles out there. Stamps, postcards, antique toys, trinkets and glassware from different eras. If your passion is Depression glass or Victorian silver, there is a market.

Maybe you are not a collector now. If this area interests you as a way to make fast money, you can get up to speed on the value and availability of certain collectibles by researching on the internet and in magazines and other publications on that particular item and area of interest.

People make great money at flea markets and antique shows and estate sales. If you know about pot belly stoves or beaded jewelry or what have you, the money is there to be made. And you can have a lot of fun in the process.

✔ **Event Tickets.** Maybe instead of stuff, you are into events. Concerts, sporting events, fighting matches, theatre, dance, etc, etc. The show must go on and somebody always needs a ticket. You can be the go-to guy.

I am not telling you to be a ticket scalper. I am suggesting that there is money to be made as a ticket reseller. It is legal most places. Don't get into trouble if it's not legal in your town!

Think of quick, easy cash. You buy tickets for the rock show coming to town and word gets out that you have the hot seats. You can advertise or you can let your friends do the vocal PR for you. Your phone will be ringing and ch-ching, you will be collecting green with no effort.

There are also lots of online opportunities to resell tickets. Some sites like StubHub are for buying and selling. Use your creativity and you will be making lots of cash in very little time.

✔ **craigslist.** The other great internet gold mine besides eBay is craigslist. There really is a guy named Craig who started an online version of a buy it/sell it bulletin board. Remember in college when people would post little notes by the campus mailbox? "Need a ride to San Diego this weekend." "Have a motorcycle to sell." "Looking for a roommate this summer?"

The concept is the same, but the venue has gone global. If you have something to offer, there is someone looking for it and they will look on craigslist. Go to www.craigslist.com and check it out. The possibilities are endless.

Sell your car, motorcycle, scooter, boat, Winnebago RV, your electronics, your jewelry, your collectibles. If you have a vacation home, rent it for a week and make big bucks fast.

If you live in New York or any other cool place that people want to visit, rent out your apartment for a week and get quick cash. It is amazing the transactions that can happen, if you use your creative mind. Think cash and think fast and it will be yours.

✔ **Take a loan against your 401(k).** If you have a nice nest egg in the retirement account and want money right here, right now, tap into the money sitting there. You get it quick, you get a good interest rate, and you are paying yourself back, not a bank.

✔ **Take a loan against other investment accounts.** Same logic applies here as well. Quick, liquid cash available when you need it. Pay back yourself at a good rate.

✔ **Cash advance on your credit card.** If you need money now, take advantage of the credit card in your wallet. You can get immediate cash in the blink of an eye.

✔ **Phone a friend.** Maybe you have a friend or relative who owes you money. Now is the time to collect. Or maybe you have a friend or relative who always offers you a loan. If you want quick cash in a jiffy, accept the loan with a heartfelt thanks. Maybe they will even give it to you interest free.

✔ **Get an advance from your employer.** Depending upon your type of work and method of payment, you may be able to get an advance from your employer. If you know you have a good commission check coming next month, take it as an advance now if you need the funds pronto.

✔ **Equity line.** If you are a homeowner, access your home equity line of credit. You can get big sums, pay little interest, and have the cash in hand with the snap of a finger.

✔ **Consult.** Find consulting jobs that pay an advance. You can use your expertise to make a quick buck. People need what you know. You need fast cash. Find a consulting job by word of mouth or online at www.csc.com, www.careerbuilder.com, and ops-jobs.theladders.com/Management-Consulting.

✔ **Licensing.** License your product or idea to an infomercial company. Infomercial companies are often willing to see you on short notice and move aggressively, if they like your product. Many are willing to pay $10–30,000 just for licensing plus a royalty. That is FAT cash FAST!

✔ **Audition.** Audition for modeling opportunities. No, not "those kind" of gigs. There are legitimate needs for print and video ads. Television commercials need local people. Maybe you can audition for acting parts as well.

✔ **Your house.** Live in a town where things happen? Super Bowl, Final Four, Olympics? Rent out your house during that week. People will pay huge money!

✔ **Think timely.** While I am on the subject of big events, sell time sensitive items when the time is hot and you can make outrageous sums of money. Sell Super Bowl champion shirts the week of the big game. Sell the big concert shirts. Use that brain and your purse will thank you.

✔ **Get a loan.** That seems like a no-brainer so we overlook the obvious. Need money fast? Get a loan from a local guy or check out the online lenders. See www.pacificadvance.com or www.bankfreedom.com/learnmore.html.

✔ **Go for the gold.** When I talk about there being a gold mine of opportunities out there for you to get quick cash, I mean it. People are having gold parties these days at their homes. Turn in your old, outdated gold jewelry (or from the last marriage) and get big money that night. You may be glad you dumped him when you see how much the loot brings you. Visit www.cash4gold.com.

Are you counting? I just gave more than ten ways. There are many more ways that I did not list. This section is to get your creative juices flowing and get you thinking of ways in your life that you can make money fast.

Any one of these ways could net you a full ten grand. Let me know what works for you and what you did that is not listed here. Your ideas could be printed in a future issue of our *Debt Cures* newsletter.

CHAPTER 14

Credit Schmedit

"Shake, rattle, and roll ..."
~Bill Haley and the Comets

We all like to think that the 1950s were the golden era of simple and innocent living. Imagine a girl in her poodle skirt at the malt shop sharing a milkshake with a guy in his letter sweater or maybe a white t-shirt and a leather jacket. It all seems so fresh, innocent, and nonthreatening. We may want to wax nostalgic for a more simple time, but the fact of the matter is those days had their not-so-happy days too.

Back to the future

Why do I have the nifty fifties on my mind? I just read an article in the *Los Angeles Times* (in May 2009, far from the 1950s) musing that the new credit card regulations coming down the pike in 2010 may have us swinging back into the tight access and low limits of the 1950s.

Folks in the 50s protected their plastic and things were a bit more conservative back then. The norm was to not rack up huge balances, to pay on time every month, and usually to pay the account in full every month.

Fast forward four or five decades, and the world is all plastic, usually all of the time, and out of control in many ways. The credit card industry is a different animal now than when it first appeared on the consumer scene in the age of seeming innocence.

Somewhere along the way, the credit card industry lost sight of being a service and convenience for its customers. It became cutthroat and greedy and secretive and sneaky. And did I mention greedy?

Times changed

The lure of easy credit ensnared many an unsuspecting consumer. The attitude shifted, and although the credit card guys did not articulate it so blatantly, the attitude became: Come, come, here is our credit card. Use it. Use it. Use it all the time, for everything and anything. Rack up charges as high as want. Pay as little as you want. Don't worry. Don't worry. Just keep using that card and using that card. Charge, charge, charge.

They tried to cast a spell over the consumers that using a credit card could solve all their problems. The credit card cads wanted to mesmerize people with the ease of use and to encourage frequent use. The encouragement of how to use credit wisely was not a part of the conversation. There was no real conversation. It was a one-sided enticement of the miraculous benefits of a new promised land, without proclaiming any of its perils.

The credit card industry should have big yellow DANGER signs. Warning: Enter at your own risk. Proceed with caution.

That is kind of what I am trying to do here and now. But the damage has been done, and we have to reverse it and move forward through the thicket of overgrown weeds and tangled webs of fraud and abuse.

Abusive practices

Over the years, the banks and credit card companies have devised more and more devious ways to get money out of the innocent credit card user. Racking up the interest rate with no fair warning—or no fair reason. Allowing charges that put the cardholder over his limit and then charging him a fee for going over. Charging a fee when a customer is given the convenience of paying her bill over the phone.

> Over the years, the banks and credit card companies have devised more and more devious ways to get money...

The list of their "crimes" goes on and on. The new legislation being bounced about in Washington aims to hit them—the credit card industry—where it hurts, but the new laws do not take effect until months and months away. I don't want to sound like a gloom and doomer, but we'll see what really takes effect at all.

If history repeats itself, then we won't see a heck of a lot happening.

Promises, promises

But the promises as of now include requiring credit card companies to give more notice before changing terms such as interest rates, and the credit card issuers won't be allowed to apply those rates retroactively to existing balances unless the cardholder's minimum payment is sixty days overdue.

If the plan sticks, they won't be allowed to charge interest on bills paid on time, they won't be able to charge extra fees for paying by phone or bank transfer, and they won't be able to issue credit cards to people under 21 without proof of income or a parent's signature.

Amen!

And credit card companies will have to apply any payment over the minimum to the balance with the highest interest. And they will not be allowed to let charges happen that put the cardholder over the credit limit and then turn around and ding them a fee for going over said limit.

You know, stuff they should have been doing all along. It is crazy that it takes drastic credit card reform to make these things happen. Let's rock around the clock and turn back the clock.

Changing times

> We're turning back the clock to the credit card of the 1960s.

Back in the fifties, most folks had a credit limit of three hundred bucks. The "elite" had a whopping five hundred bucks. My, my, times have changed.

The American Bankers Association is already freaking out and crying to anyone who will listen. One spokesman from the banker boys said, "Some people will not be able to get a credit card that got it in the past, and those who get the credit card, in some instances, will have a smaller line of credit. We're turning back the clock to the credit card of the 1960s. Everybody paid $25 a year and was charged 18% and it was a very straightforward card, but a lot of people couldn't qualify, the lines of credit were smaller and those who handled credit well subsidized those with credit issues."

The blowhard bankers are crying in their soup and we don't care. We know that they are the ones who turned the tables over the years and turned the credit card industry into the crazed world that it has become. They don't care about their customers. All they care about is their profits.

We know it. They know it. Stop the baloney.

The pot called the kettle ...

I'm not the one calling the kettle black. Well, yeah, I guess I am. I'm also the bearer of the news and the experts are the ones who back me up.

Robert D. Manning, director of a consumer financial center at the Rochester Institute of Technology, said in this *LA Times* interview: "In the old industrial economy, the best client was one who could pay off debts. In the post-industrial economy, the best customer is the person who can't pay it off."

The bankers and the credit card companies are bloodsuckers, and they fear that their supply of blood will dry up if new regulations get put into play.

Another typical story

A "good citizen/bad banker" story in this particular article shows my point. One innocent credit card user got his first piece of plastic in college. They gave him an expensive textbook to get him to sign up.

Here we have a hard-working medical student who paid his bill on time every month. The credit card company kept increasing his credit limit and our boy thought things were just fine.

His credit limit was $8,000. Think about it. He was a student, a poor student from a low-income neighborhood. He is spending all his time in class where he is not making money. Would you give him an $8,000 loan? How in the world can he repay?

Talk about taking advantage.

His Credit Card Company jacked his interest rate from 7.99% to 15.99%. Our student was aghast. He made his payments on time every month. So he called. What did he learn? That he was screwed.

Tightened the screws even more

He was told that since he was nearing the top of his credit limit, they were increasing his interest rate. Yes, the credit limit that they had continually jacked up while they continually took his on-time monthly payments. He thought he had been rewarded for being a good customer with these credit line increases. Wrong.

Just another tactic the credit card companies use to get more money.

Our Mr. Med Student was told that they had sent him a letter telling him about the interest rate increase. He never received the letter. Every month he paid $90, his minimum payment, and thought the world was just fine.

With the rate increase, his monthly payment jumped to $200. Then the fees started piling up, $39 for over-the-limit. Gee, what happened to upping his limit every few months?

It gets worse. Mr. Med Student was not working to pay the higher payment and couldn't do it. It all snowballed and the next thing he knew, his minimum payment skyrocketed to over $600 a month.

Gimme a break!

Unbelievable but true

Now it really gets worse. The credit card bank then raised his rate again! If they would have left him alone, he would have been just fine. Now because of their shenanigans, he is over his head in credit card debt.

His rate was jacked to 24.99%, a far cry from where he started. Waiting on his student loan check in order to pay his bills, Mr. Med Student missed a credit card payment that month. The bank hits him with more fees and his new monthly minimum payment became $990—almost a grand!

It would be laughable, but it's no joke. It's real. And this guy is just one story among millions. He had a minimum payment of ninety bucks and then it becomes nine hundred dollars more. Come on!

This guy maintains that he would have been okay if they had left his rate alone. I believe him. He was a good customer. He made his payment every month, on time. How did he get rewarded? They hung him out to dry.

Cowards and crooks

What makes the story ever so real is that the coward bankers hide. If they believed that their practices were sound, they would be in the media defending themselves. They know they are in the wrong. When asked to comment on this one incident, they refused.

The Credit Card Company used the pat answer that they can't discuss private accounts because of customer privacy. Yes, we all know how much they care about their customers.

The bankers and credit card companies are bellowing that if new regulations come down, that means tighter rules and interest rates for everyone will go higher. No logic there, they just want to blame someone else, and they want you and me to blame someone else. God forbid we place blame where it is due, squarely on their shoulders.

Blame game

The banks and the credit card issuers always want to put the blame on the consumer and the spending habits of we, the people. We know better. The *LA Times* backed me up. They talked to Elizabeth Warren, a Harvard Law School professor, who we quoted in the first *Debt Cures* book.

From the *Los Angeles Times*: "Research conducted by a team including Elizabeth Warren, a Harvard Law School professor and consumer debt expert, suggests that people who fall into serious debt tend to do so because of a harsh roll of the dice—job loss, illness, divorce—and not profligate spending."

She concurs with what we've known all along. "This is not that people go out each month and buy too many iPods or other crazy things," said Warren, whose 2001 study was based on an analysis of bankruptcy filings. "It's that they spent so much of their salary on the basics—mortgage, child care, college tuition, health insurance, whatever—that month after month they end up short on day-to-day living. They can't do it anymore."

> He also made it clear that the disaster is due to the practices of the credit card industry.

People are using credit just to get by. And the "friendly" credit card provider has turned into a two-faced evil clown. I think of the bad witch in *The Wizard of Oz*. She says, "Here, here, my pretty," but she doesn't want to help; she only wants the ruby slippers. The bankers will say anything, but they will steal the sneakers off your feet.

I never promised you a rose garden

President Obama made a Rose Garden ceremony out of the signing of the new law. The credit card world is far from a rose garden. It is thorny though. He said credit card companies have "made it difficult" for folks who carry a balance on their accounts and are trying to get out of debt. That is the understatement of the year.

The Prez said that many people got trapped when the economy tanked. How true. He also made it clear that the disaster is due to the practices of the credit card industry. Millions of folks are over their heads in credit card debt. It's not because these millions of folks spend every weekend hanging out at the mall.

Some of the practices that were targeted include those that we have been targeting: the confusing fine print, the sudden appearance of unexplained fees on bills, the sudden change in payment due dates, the sudden increase in interest rates for no reason, and how the credit card gurus take your money and apply it to the low interest portion first instead of the balance that has the higher interest rate.

Same old story

If you want to read the entire *Los Angeles Times* article, you can read it online at www.latimes.com/business/la-fi-credit26-2009may26,0,5507218.story. You could spend a lifetime online reading all the stories of how the credit card companies rip off the little guy. And pretend that they don't.

Who do they think they're fooling? Not me. And I know, not you.

CHAPTER 15

Ways to Pay

"Can we do it? Yes we can!"

~Bob the Builder

Life is meant to be enjoyed. Love may be forever, but credit card debt should not be. Call it temporary insanity if you want, but we should NOT be paying those credit card bills until death do us part.

Industry insider

The money experts tell me what to do and I do it and I tell you. I don't proclaim to be an expert, but I am much more than a talking head. I know this stuff, I was an industry insider years ago, and I know what they do. "They" are not people I associate with anymore. I am a regular guy on the streets who knows a lot and needs to share it.

I also know that what we here at the Debt Cures team say is great advice. Helpful ways to get you out of debt and on with your life. And if you come across a new way to cure the debt and create the wealth, send it on to us to share with other readers.

There is also simply having a book like this to give you that little nudge, that kick in the pants to get off the couch and take back control of your financial situation and your life. Just because the government

135

and the credit card companies are sticking it to you does not mean you have to just lie there and take it.

Fight back

Some of what I preach is common sense. It still makes sense and should be put into practice. I will assume that you have credit card debt on several credit cards. Most Americans have thousands in debt and have many cards in use.

There is more than one way to skin a cat (my apologies, animal lovers), and there is more than one way to tackle the credit card bills.

Financial gurus suggest different ways to regain control of your finances. It is up to you to decide what you prefer.

Pick a card

The accelerated payment method is exactly that. Take a look at all your credit card balances and the interest rates. Pick the account that has the highest interest rate and concentrate on getting that card paid off.

Keep making at least the minimum payment on all your other cards, but this one is your targeted attack. Make big chunks of payment on it every month. Because it has the highest rate, it is the one that is costing you the most. The longer you carry a balance, the more wasted dough on interest charges.

Use the ways that I tell you about how to raise quick cash and use such quick cash to pay down the high interest card. When this account balance gets paid off, the relief and sense of accomplishment that you will feel is unmatched.

It gives you the confidence to tackle the next account with the next highest interest rate. A lot of what happens in *Debt Cures* is about giving you the confidence to take control of your financial situation.

You are in this mess due to no fault of your own, but there is no sense playing the victim. Fighting back is strengthening.

Any card

This accelerated repayment method is simply focusing on one account balance with more laser focus and more cash to get it off your plate. Besides the highest interest, some people prefer to go after the account that has the largest balance.

Maybe you have three cards all hovering around a thousand dollars and one that is at five grand. You decide to set your sights on the five grand and get it knocked off. Same theory. When it is paid off, you get to cross it off your list and do a happy dance in your kitchen. Then you go after the next highest balance, and off you go.

> This accelerated repayment method is simply focusing on one account balance.

For some people, they need quicker results to bring about that sense of achievement and give the encouragement to keep marching on. For them, it is often suggested to pick the lowest credit card balance. Pay it off.

The very reality of having it gone does wonders for the self esteem. One less bill to pay next month is very freeing. It removes the burden and makes the whole get out of debt concept seem possible.

Some of you have been living with debt for so long that you can't imagine a different reality. That is why this method helps. It changes your reality in a tangible way. One less check to write this month, having that balance PAID IN FULL is freeing, and can spur you on to greater financial heights.

The house

Depending upon your situation, one option to knocking off those pesky credit card bills overnight is to tap into your house. That could mean digging up the hordes of cash you buried in the yard or, if you don't have that, you can use the equity line and pay off the high interest credit card accounts.

This is not a fail-safe method. You need to be able to make the mortgage payment and the home equity repayment, but the equity line most often has a much better interest rate than any credit card. And you are paying yourself back. I like you much better than the credit card companies.

If you are not planning on staying in your house for a while, this may not make sense for you. So only you know what is right for you.

Negotiate

When talking about debt elimination, one factor that always needs to be brought up is negotiation. You have a big pile of debt and you want it gone. The quickest way to have it gone would be if it were a smaller pile of debt. Make sense?

The best way and the quickest way to get the debt pile down is the ancient art of negotiation. Put your money where your mouth is. Or use your mouth to put money back in your pockets.

Pick up the phone and do what we have talked about. Explain your situation and how you want to make this debt go away. Explain that you want to pay, but you need them to meet you in the middle. Explain that you are trying to avoid bankruptcy and that if you went that route, they would not get paid at all.

They want some money. You want to pay some money. You just don't want to pay all the interest and penalty charges that have been racked up, for example. Negotiate paying the principle balance and having the creditor wipe away the other fees.

Money talks

Negotiate whatever you want, however you want. Different tactics work for different people, and every situation is different. Maybe you are Nice Guy and don't have it in you to raise your voice. Maybe you are Hard Ball Negotiator and have no qualms taking on the big dogs.

In this time and this economy, you've got nothing to lose and everything to gain. Get rid of the pile of bricks and the weight off your shoulders. Ask and you shall receive.

Don't forget to have your creditors wipe off any negative items from your credit report as well. They can do that. They can eliminate collection activity, so be sure to throw that nugget into your talks.

Imagine having the debt gone and the "bad marks" off your credit report. Your improved credit score will impact your life. Instead of feeling the negative, it can all be positive. The weight can be lifted off your shoulders. All you need to do is negotiate it.

It really works

One gentleman I know, Joel, applied the simple art of negotiation and his debt went from topping out at around $50,000 all the way down to $13,000. He is a *Debt Cures* success story. Joel wiped out most of his debt and now he is driving a $100,000 Mercedes! Take that, bill collectors!

Make a statement

A great *Debt Cures* tip is to show the lenders that your net worth is not that of a multi millionaire and that you simply cannot pay.

How do you show lenders that they need to work with you? Put it in black and white. Your current net worth can show that you have no more resources to pay what they are asking of you. Take your personal financial statements to the bank or lender or collector: "You can squeeze all you want, but the well is dry. You can't get something that doesn't exist and my means to pay does not exist."

> They would rather get a little something than nothing at all.

When they see that you are tapped out, so to speak, they usually are more willing to make a quick negotiation.

A simple balance sheet and income statement are easy enough to do on your own. You can also hire a local accountant or use your "phone a friend" option. If you have a friend who is an accountant or lawyer, they can draft a letter for you on their letterhead that simply states you have no ability to pay. With such a letter, the creditors are more willing to negotiate with you. They would rather get a little something than nothing at all.

The debt collector will see your financial statements and read your letter, which states very plainly: *this is my net worth, consisting of these assets — my house, my cars, and my wedding rings; these liabilities: mortgage loan debt, car loan debt, credit card debt #1, credit card debt #2, student loan debt, etc.* After looking at this, your creditors should be more accessible and more realistic in their demands. For example, they won't keep insisting that you pay the whole $80,000 that you owe if it is clear that all you could ever pay is $10,000. And maybe all you can pay is nothing. If you have a negative net worth, show it.

Money talks. And no money may make them walk.

CHAPTER 16

Smart Plays

"You have brains in your head ..."

~Dr. Seuss

Obviously you have brains in your head or you would not be reading this book. You did the right thing by investing in yourself with the simple purchase of this tome of helpful hints for better living. Sound like Martha Stewart, don't I?

Getting out of debt is indeed the path to better living. You are already on the path. Congratulations.

Now to keep you on the path, follow the trail of crumbs or the signs posted on the trees or follow the North Star or...Just read this book.

Do what you can

As you know, I HATE FEES. So my advice is do whatever is in your power to avoid them. The banks and the credit card companies do what they can to jab you with fees; you need to do what you can to avoid the stick.

I see stories all the time of single moms struggling to get by and the darn credit card companies hit them with fees and make paying the bills an even bigger burden. We know the stories. Lunch and coffee put on the charge card made the over limit buzzer go off down at the credit card place.

One small charge for the lady. One huge resulting pile of fees from the credit card company. The banks will clear these charges when you use your debit card and without you knowing, you have dropped below zero. Instead of rejecting the card and saying overdraft, the purchase goes through.

And a few days later—after you have continued to use the card for more small purchases—you get notice that you have insufficient funds. What's wrong with this picture? My real question is what's wrong with them?!

Get notified

Do your best to avoid the fees by getting the alerts that can be set up on your account. It is too easy to overdraw our accounts these days because the banks WANT us to! They want to hit us up with fees.

I know of one gal who ran up $400 in fees because she was not aware that she had overdrawn. That, in a word, is wrong. Most people today are on very tight budgets and $400 in fees is $400 that seems like $4,000.

Besides keeping tabs on your account balance, online, at an ATM machine, and over the phone, take the extra step. Most banks have an "alert" system. You set a specified amount and when your account hits that dollar figure, you are notified. You should set the alert for higher than zero so you know before you drop below.

Automatic help

Many banks have automatic overdraft protection that you can sign up for. If your account dips into the negative, funds from another account or equity line will be transferred to cover the balance.

There may be a small fee for this service. This fee is usually better than a single overdraft charge.

Banks launched a whole new gig for themselves by letting overdrafts happen and then charging customers for it. What a blatant ripoff and lack of ethics.

"No comment"

A recent class action lawsuit brought this to light. A certain Bank settled for $35 million because they were accused of allowing overdrafts, and indeed manipulating what charges cleared an account first in order for the overdraft to happen, and then socking it to their customers in fees.

> They think they are crafty, but eventually, the truth always wins out.

The Bank denied the charges but yet they settled for $35 MILLION! You tell me, what's the real story? Yeah, we know who is up to no good. The good old bank pleads "no comment."

Another similar case happened with Washington Mutual, which has since been acquired. The acquiring bank also declines comment on any pending action. The silence is deafening. They think they are crafty, but eventually, the truth always wins out.

The numbers don't lie

The fee racket is just that and it is huge money. That is why the banks do it, of course. They are looking for new ways all the time to put the squeeze on the American citizen, and overdraft fees alone are unbelievable.

The Center for Responsible Lending states that the amount of actual overdraws is $15 billion. Guess how much the banks charge in fees? $17.5 BILLION! They charge more than the amount that people are actually dipping below. What a racket!

Think about it. Have you ever gone below zero? Sure. Let's say the bank cleared a debit card charge and you went ten bucks in the hole. For that measly ten bucks, they charge you $39 for it! Gimme a break! And they do that enough to people that they rake in $17.5 BILLION in overdraft penalty fees!

The FDIC states that half of all overdrafts are from debit charges and ATM withdrawals, all small amounts. Not only are they small amounts and getting hit with huge fees, the very nature of the ATM and debit card technology is to stay on top of the account balance. One should always know their standing and not be blindsided by a greedy bank's attempt to extract a fee.

Fees are stupid

These stupid overdraft fees hurt us, the good citizens, and the overall economy. This following statement makes great sense to me. I read it in USA Today, a customer who agrees that these fees are stupid: "It's ridiculous that the very banks that we're bailing out as taxpayers are charging us $35 for each overdraft. That's money I could be dumping back into the economy." (Source: www.usatoday.com/money/industries/banking/2009-03-22-bank-overdraft-fees_N.htm)

This article was posted online, and some of the comments were eye opening and exactly what we are talking about. This is what one consumer said:

Bank of America has taken overdraft fees to a new level. Now Bank of America charges an Overdraft Fee if the "Pending Balance" goes into a negative, even though the actual account balance is still positive. Even though the bank has not yet "PAID" the item.

In other words, the pending item has not posted to the account, so the account balance is still positive, but the pending balance is negative, so Bank of America charges a $35 overdraft fee.

My example would be a pending watch repair charge that took my pending balance on Monday, 04/27, to a negative balance, but because of the watch company's merchant services, the item did not post to the account until 04/29. At no time did my actual balance drop below zero, but because my pending balance on Monday, 04/27, dropped below zero, Bank of America charged my account a $35 overdraft fee.

I did not write a comment, but this next person is right after my own heart. Calling them "banking pirates"—I love it! I agree!

… these banking pirates, but they are. For decades, banks have declined credit card purchases at the Point of Sale when limits were exceeded … and at NO charge, just perhaps a little embarrassment. But then some creative marketing guy saw a windfall of profits with debit cards, to spare us the embarrassment of a "decline," which has evolved into a license to steal, or at best, extortion.

Let's see … how about one more …

On the street, these practices are illegal and you go to prison. It's called loan sharking, extortion, robbery, etc. The banks call these practices "courtesies" … AHHHHH, I get it, a gesture of good will!!, save the fact that you just screwed me out of $35 over a 1 cent error, netting you a whopping 3500% profit in a single 24 hour period!!

I could not have said it better myself. You can read all the comments from people just like you at www.usatoday.com/money/industries/banking/2009-03-22-bank-overdraft-fees_N.htm.

What about your bank?

2009 USA TODAY bank overdraft survey

A *USA TODAY* survey of the 10 largest retail banks, by assets, in the nation found that nine process paychecks and electronic transactions from highest to lowest dollar amount. SunTrust, which declined to respond to the survey, says in its deposit agreement that it will pay transactions in any order it likes, including from "largest to smallest dollar amount." Other results of the survey:

Largest retail banks[1]	Ability to overdraw at ATM	Ability to overdraw online	Ability to overdraw at point of sale	Warning given for ATM overdraft	Warning for point of sale overdraft[2]	Overdraft fee amount
Bank of America	Yes	Yes	Yes	Yes	No	$35
JPMorgan Chase	Yes[3]	Yes	Yes	NA	No	$25 $35
Citigroup	No	Yes[4]	No	NA	NA	$34
Wells Fargo	Yes	Yes	Yes	Yes	No	$35[5]
HSBC North America[6]	Yes	Yes	Yes	Yes	No	$35
PNC Financial Services[6]	Yes	Yes	Yes	Yes	No	$31 $36
U.S. Bancorp	Yes	Yes	Yes	Yes	No	$19 $37.50
SunTrust	-	-	-	-	-	$25 $36[7]
Capital One[6]	Yes	Yes	Yes	No	No	$35
Citizens Financial	Yes	Yes	Yes	No	No	$22 $39

1 - banks generally calculate overdrafts based on once-a-day transaction processing; 2 - banks generally say the merchants' processing system doesn't allow them to warn consumers of point-of-sale overdraft; 3 - bank will decline ATM transactions if the consumer doesn't have sufficient funds, but end-of-the-day processing means those ATM transactions could later overdraw account; 4 - ACH transfers may overdraw account; 5- in most states; 6 - customers can tell banks not to pay certain *overdrafts;* 7- information from bank's online fee schedule; fee will rise to $36 on May 1. *Sources: USA TODAY* research, bank information

Source: www.usatoday.com/money/industries/banking/2009-03-22-bank-overdraft-fees_N.htm.

More sources

Remember the old commercial slogan, "Choosy moms choose Jif"? Well, your choice of credit card is more important than your choice of peanut butter. But if you are making me a sandwich, I prefer crunchy. And lots of jelly.

If you are shopping for a credit card, be a sleuth and get what you want. Do not pay fees. Do not agree to a high interest rate. Don't fall for a low teaser introductory rate if the regular rate after that time period is up is going to be high. Make sure that balance transfer fees do not apply or are reasonable.

At the risk of sounding like a broken record, be diligent in your efforts to get the best rate. If you sign up for the teaser rate and they send you a card with a different rate because your credit is not so great, cancel the card.

If the intro rate is great but the balance transfer fee is high, think first. Get out the calculator and ballpark the numbers. Maybe to transfer $1000 to a new card will cost you $40. Is that really saving you any money in the big scheme of things? Crunch your figures before you go leaping.

> If there is no grace period, you don't really want that card.

Credit cards always used to offer a 30-day grace period. That means you had thirty days to pay the balance before any interest accrued. Now, the grace period is much less, usually twenty days, and some cards don't give you any. If there is no grace period, you don't really want that card.

And I can't say it enough—know what your limit is and don't get close to it. If you go even a penny over the credit limit, the fee is slapped with a mighty THUMP. Do you really want to face a $39 charge?

Search

To search for the right card for you, use the mighty internet. Some sites are better than others. I do not get a kickback for naming any, but I will suggest www.cardratings.com. They offer updated information and articles and news you can use about what is going on in the credit card industry.

This is the most comprehensive free source to compare over 500 different credit cards. This site posts reviews—like over 20,000 reviews—so you can read what others have experienced and what advice they have to give.

Pretty cool.

And more

Another source I can recommend to you, especially if you are trying to get a credit card while you are in the process of improving your credit score, is www.credit.com. Take a peek at www.credit.com/products/credit_cards/sub-prime.jsp. This section features credit cards for people with bad credit.

May I remind you, never say never.

There are credit cards and prepaid cards for those of you who are struggling and want to get back or create good credit. Where there is a will, there's a way, and a credit card.

This site is easy to navigate. They offer different card types depending on what you are looking for, for example, low APR, secured cards, or student cards. If you want the best deal on balance transfers, give it a click. Looking for cash back cards, air miles, gas cards? Click, click, click.

They also break it down by credit score so you can search for the best card depending upon where you fall in the score numbers:

Excellent = 750+
Good = 700–749
Fair = 650–699
Poor = 600–649
Bad = Below 599

They even have a link for No Credit. It is worthwhile to know your credit score and know where that places you in the credit world. The better the score, the better card deal you are able to get.

And still more

Another helpful internet site is www.creditcards.com. This is another free site that shows various credit cards and what they offer and what they charge. You can search for low interest credit cards and use the side-by-side tool to compare them.

Very handy.

They give their top pick and provide the contact info if you want to apply for any of the cards. You can start the process with a simple click.

I know of another site for those who need a card and have credit trouble. Go to www.newhorizon.org/Info/unsecured.htm.

At newhorizon.org, they list unsecured credit cards for people with bad credit. These cards do not require money down like secured cards. Sometimes with bad credit, the idea is to reestablish credit, so you put down a deposit and receive a card in that amount.

These cards at this site are unsecured, like a "normal" credit card. So even if you have bad credit, you can get a card with no money down. These cards report to the credit reporting agencies and that is how you work your way back to good credit. Make regular monthly on-time payments. Each month that gets generated into the credit report.

Be aware that you may have to pay a fee for this process.

Check out these sites if you are shopping for credit cards. The choices are many. Choose wisely. (And choose whatever peanut butter you want.)

CHAPTER 17

Foreclosures

"What a tangled web we weave,
when first we practice to deceive."

~Sir Walter Scott

Have no sympathy for the web weavers. They spun this mess and we are the ones tangled up in it. The number of people losing their homes is millions and still happening. The banks have never had so many foreclosed properties. They don't know what to do with them. (Oh, pity the poor banks.)

We are making history all right, and it ain't pretty.

Lies and deceit

The Associated Press reported in late April 2009 that the CEO of one of the big mortgage companies agreed to pay fines of almost 2.5 million bucks to settle charges of fraud amid the mortgage meltdown. I guess hangin's too good for some people.

Here is the scoop straight from the news, not me (but the bold emphasis is mine):

By MARCY GORDON, AP Business Writer —Tue Apr 28, 2009

The former head of American Home Mortgage Investment Corp. has agreed to pay nearly $2.5 million to settle federal civil charges of accounting fraud and concealing the company's deteriorating finances as the subprime mortgage crisis hit in 2007.

The Securities and Exchange Commission announced the settlement Tuesday with former American Home Chairman and Chief Executive Michael Strauss, the company's founder.

Charges against the company's former chief financial officer, Stephen Hozie, also accused of accounting fraud and misleading investors, are pending. The SEC also alleged that Strauss, Hozie and former controller Robert Bernstein misled American Home's auditor about the adequacy of the company's reserves against losses on mortgages.

Carl Loewenson, Jr., an attorney representing Hozie, declined to comment Tuesday, as did Bernstein's attorney, Frank Wohl. Strauss's lawyer, Peter Bresnan, didn't return calls seeking comment.

The executives were major players in the national mortgage meltdown, an SEC official said. *American Home filed for bankruptcy protection in August 2007 and is currently in the process of liquidating. It fell from being one of the nation's 10 biggest mortgage lenders to insolvency in about a week, as its lenders demanded more collateral for their loans.*

Like scores of other mortgage companies, Melville, N.Y.-based American Home was left with no capital to operate as the market for securities tied to high-risk subprime home loans dried up after a spike in homeowner defaults. ***The collapse in the mortgage-backed bonds in 2007 helped set off the global economic crisis.***

Strauss, 50, who lives in Southampton, N.Y., ***neither admitted or denied wrongdoing in his settlement*** *with the SEC, though he did agree to refrain from future violations of securities laws. He* *agreed to pay about $2.2 million in restitution and interest, and a $250,000 civil fine. Strauss also will be barred for five years from serving as an officer or director of any public company.*

In a civil lawsuit filed in federal court in Manhattan, the SEC alleged that Strauss and Hozie fraudulently understated American Home's reserves against losses on home loans by tens of millions of dollars for the first quarter of 2007. They knew the company needed at least another $38 million in reserves and made the loss into a "fictional profit." The two executives also deceived investors about the company's financial condition and the riskiness of the home loans it made, according to the agency.

"These senior executives did not just occupy a front row seat to the mortgage meltdown—they were part of the show," *SEC Enforcement Director Robert Khuzami said in a statement. "As the housing market imploded, these executives kept secret that the company's holdings were collapsing like a house of cards."*

The SEC has said it is investigating about two dozen cases related to possible mortgage fraud, in addition to its efforts with the Justice Department and other federal agencies.

"The investigation into mortgage-related fraud is a high priority," Khuzami said Tuesday in a telephone interview. "We intend to aggressively pursue" those cases.

The Senate voted Tuesday to hire hundreds more FBI agents and federal prosecutors to investigate the roughly 5,000 allegations of mortgage fraud that come in every month. *The $530 million provided in the legislation would enable hiring of an additional 160 special FBI agents and more than 200 support staff over two years; it also includes $40 million to boost the SEC's enforcement staff.*

*Strauss and Hozie **failed to disclose** to investors that American Home was forced to sell the bulk of its multibillion-dollar holdings* *of mortgage-linked securities in April 2007 to meet pressing needs for cash flow, the SEC alleged in its suit. **Most of the company's home loans in 2006 were made without verifying the borrower's income,** the agency said.*

(Source: *www.nytimes.com/2009/04/29/business/29lend.html*)

Holy smokes! Need the Cliffs Notes version of that article?

CEO of big mortgage bank = greedy bad guy who did not tell the truth.

Enron was the start, is there no end?

> Corporate greed is at epidemic proportions.

A few years ago, it would be hard to believe that the bankers and mortgage lenders could act in such a despicable way, but we see it over and over again now. The proof is before our very eyes. Corporate greed is at epidemic proportions. Out of control and reckless.

And all the countless people who lost their homes, what happens to them? Do they get a share of that $2.2 million that this guy agreed to pay—even though, of course, he admits no wrongdoing? Where's the justice for them?

The little guy won't see one thin dime.

The homeowners probably wish for their proverbial day in court. As would the investors in this company who also were screwed.

Intent to mislead

Let's see, SEC charges of misleading investors and accounting fraud and "fictional profits," and the guy does not go to jail. I find it disgusting. The secrets, lies, and deceit would make for a good

Hollywood movie, except we all know the plot and the ending, and frankly, the story is getting old.

The SEC (Securities Exchange Commission) also stated that "most of the company's home loans in 2006 were made without verifying the borrower's income." That comment warrants a good slap on the head with a Homer Simpson, "DOH!"

Hmm, business school basics would seem to teach that before you give a loan, you find out the person's income and the ability to pay back the loan. It seems like common sense, but common sense can take a leave of absence when greed takes over.

Greed is not good

The bigwigs wanted money, plain and simple. They did whatever they wanted and gave out loans to folks who in reality needed credit counseling, not a mortgage that was too big for them to afford. The execs had no interest in anything but lining their own pockets. Now our economy is in shambles, people are homeless, and it all started with the home loan guys like this CEO bozo.

The feds stepped in, but so far it seems to be too little, too late. Certainly, too late. Time will tell what the government under President Obama will do, but right now, there are no miracles being pulled out of any hats.

A government program has been created called Hope for Homeowners. In July of 2008, Congress passed this so-called housing rescue plan. The plan was to guarantee up to $300 billion worth of mortgages and to prevent more than 300,000 foreclosures.

This was, of course, after hundreds of thousands of foreclosures had already taken place. The plan was intended to be a stop-gap measure. But to participate, banks have to take steep losses and their participation is voluntary.

Gee, what a great plan.

Hope for regulations?

How about a little bit of regulation that forces the banks to comply? How about a little bit of regulation in the beginning that would have noticed that the banks were handing out bogus loans? How about a little bit of brains, compassion, or common sense?

No surprise, but the Hope for Homeowners plan is not looking too hopeful as we go to print. The word has not gotten out to the general public, and not many applications have been filed since the deal started October 1, 2008. In early January 2009, not a single loan had been worked out through this program. It should be renamed Little Hope for Homeowners.

What if you are among the vast number of people in America who are facing foreclosure or are having trouble making the mortgage payment? Don't despair. Obviously, you are far from being alone.

I have some new Debt Cures to bring you aid.

Show me

The first new technique is three magic words: Produce the note.

I'm telling you, these magic words that I share with you throughout my books are amazing, and bring results. Three little words—produce the note—can make the difference between keeping your home and losing it.

This is how it works. The banks enter into mortgages with customers like you and then they sell off the mortgages in bundles to mortgage service companies or another bank or investment house.

That actual piece of paper called your mortgage can get lost in the shuffle somewhere. The holder of your mortgage account may not actually hold your note. Even if they do not have the physical document, they start foreclosure proceedings and you feel the pinch.

Pinch back.

If they don't have the piece of paper documenting that you indeed owe, you have bought yourself some time and a little time may be all you need. The courts are buried with foreclosure cases. Most judges do not want to be bothered with the ones that are hassles. They want to rubber stamp the proceeding. If you show up and demand that the lender produce the note, the stall tactic can give you several more months. The judge would prefer to work a cut and dry case, so ones with "obstacles"—like you demanding the note—may very well be delayed.

Delay tactics can work

While the mortgage holder is searching through the mountains of mortgages to find your note, you can be working your systems to find any way possible to raise the funds to pay on your mortgage and get caught up.

Does this tactic mean that you don't have to pay your mortgage? No. It means that the foreclosure proceedings of your case can be shelved for a few months. Time is on your side. I have read about this cure and have seen reports on the news, and it has worked for many, many people. It may be the ticket you need to keep your home.

Judge not

Besides the "produce the note" tip, the judges are getting tired of all the foreclosures and are taking a hard look at the paperwork that crosses their bench. There's a lot of shoddy paperwork being thrown together by the foreclosure companies and it is not passing the muster of some judges.

That is a good thing.

If the judge thinks the paperwork is incomplete or inaccurate, he or she can dismiss your foreclosure proceeding. According to a report by the *Wall Street Journal*, judges all across the country are taking their time and giving the documents a thorough look.

> ...judges... are taking their time and giving the documents a thorough look.

If there are mistakes, the judge does not have to accept the case. There is one judge in Brooklyn who has dismissed dozens of cases because of sloppy paperwork and suspicions that things are not quite right.

This guy throws out the iffy cases, and not many of them make it back to court because they are not proper or legit. Good news for the homeowners. Judge Arthur Schack told the paper, "Taking away someone's home is a serious matter. I'm a neutral party and in reviewing papers filed with the court, I have to make sure they're proper."

Thank goodness there are still some good judges on the bench. Read about them at blogs.wsj.com/law/2008/07/25/subprime-legal-judges-scrutinize-mortgage-docs-deny-foreclosures/.

The foreclosure business got out of hand. These judges had the sense to make sure it all was handled properly and they were finding out that a lot of foreclosures were a targeted ripoff of the home-owner.

Red flags

The main red flags that the judges found were that all these mortgage-related companies were, in fact, housed at the same address. Hmm. Something smells like a rat. And if it smells like a rat, it usually is.

Employees were working both sides of the deal and signing affidavits stating otherwise. It was like a real two-face. "Hi, let me give you a mortgage. Now let me turn around and show my other face—the one who will take the house away from you."

What happens to TwoFace in the Batman movies? I hope he gets pulverized.

Papers were also a little shady. Mortgage assignments were backdated. Basically the mortgage/foreclosure guys were playing games with the paperwork. It was a game to them and look what happened. We all lost.

Thankfully, some foreclosures were snuffed out because of careful judges. If you are facing foreclosure, make sure the attorney involved or whoever is helping you asks that all paperwork be scrutinized.

If things are amiss, it is highly likely that your case could be dismissed. That is not a stall tactic. That is a way to keep your home.

Talk to someone

If you are facing foreclosure, and you have nowhere else to turn, go to your local HUD office. They can steer you to a counselor, for free, who can help you sort it all out. To find the office nearest you, go to www.hud.gov.

Walk away

Who would have thought it possible that a homeowner would just walk away from their home? It is happening now.

CNN reports that some folks are taking a look at their mortgage payments that they can't afford, looking at the value of their home that has declined, and doing what a few years ago would have been unthinkable. They leave.

They leave the house. They leave the mortgage. They go to the mortgage lender and hand over the keys.

A new world

Many people bought their homes with little or no money down. They are not leaving a huge nest egg of equity. They are leaving a headache that they can no longer afford. If they were able to sell, they would not get what they paid and would not be able to pay off the mortgage balance.

There is no sense or cents in paying a huge house payment on a house that is no longer worth what you paid for it. People cannot make the mortgage payment, so they take the hit on the credit score instead of spending thousands and thousands of dollars to still end up in a negative situation.

> They are leaving a headache that they can no longer afford.

A spokesman for the FICO folks said this makes sense and is a better alternative than going broke and filing bankruptcy. "Credit scores are hurt much more by missing multiple payments—on credit cards, cars and so on—than by a single foreclosure. The time it takes to regain your credit score [after fore-closure] can be shorter than after bankruptcy." (Source: money.cnn.com/2008/02/06/real_estate/walking_away/index.htm.)

Stranger than fiction

It sort of seems like science fiction, but the CNN report is fact:

It typically takes three years of a spotless payment record after a bankruptcy before credit scores recover enough for someone to think about buying a home again. After abandoning a mortgage, a person may be able to buy a new house in two years or less.

And now skipping out on a home is easier, thanks to the Mortgage Debt Relief Act of 2007. Previously, if a bank sold a foreclosed home for less than the mortgage balance and it forgave the difference, the borrower had to pay tax on that difference as if it were income. Now the IRS will ignore it.

(Source: money.cnn.com/2008/02/06/real_estate/walking_away/index.htm)

Now you have another option to consider: Walking away.

CHAPTER 18

Make $ From Foreclosures

"Show me the money!"

~ Jerry McGuire

As with all things in life, there is a downside and an upside. The upside to this foreclosure frenzy is that you can actually make money during these crazy times. In fact, you can make big money.

As you know, foreclosures are at an all-time high. The banks want to unload these properties. People who are struggling to make their house payments want to sell. It is a buyer's market. Prices have never been better.

How low can you go?

What is standard investment strategy? Buy low.

How low?

Hang on to your hats, but houses are selling for less than a thousand bucks. Unbelievable! But believe it. Truth is stranger than fiction. There are houses going dirt cheap all across the country.

You may have seen some news reports stating the deals in your state or maybe even in your town. There are literally hundreds of bargains to be had. Most of these foreclosure properties are what are called "fixer uppers." No worries there. If you are handy or even if you are not, you can make a wise purchase and make a profit that will astound you.

Even if you pay for the repairs, remodeling, or rehab, the prices that you can purchase at mean that you still walk away with a hefty gain. Use the realty websites like www.realtor.com or www.zillow.com to find inexpensive properties. Find something in your price range and get a good estimate of what fixing it up will cost.

For example, maybe you can find a house and buy it for three thousand dollars. Even if you do a lot of the handy work yourself and hire some out, let's assume you end up paying twenty grand in rehab expenses. If you turn around and sell the property for $50,000, you have doubled your money! Doubling your money! That is a return on investment that appeals to everybody!

How high can profits go?

Profits can be even greater than that. There are low cost homes everywhere and not necessarily in low cost neighborhoods. People of all income brackets have faced foreclosure. Homes with $300,000 mortgages and the homeowners could not make the payments, and ended up losing their homes.

The foreclosure crisis affected all income brackets, all education levels, all races, all areas, all states. Which means opportunities are everywhere.

You can get into a high-end area and buy some properties at prices that were unheard of just a couple years back. I know of guys who are buying these upper crust homes at rock bottom prices and selling some and making some rental properties. Lots of former homeowners are renters these days. They are used to a certain type of home, but getting a mortgage can be tougher now so they are renting.

Yes, you can

You can take advantage of the current situation and make a fortune off of foreclosures. Don't feel guilty about it. You and I did not create this mess. The good old boys in Washington and the fat cat bankers can take the credit for this situation.

Don't get me started on those fat cat bankers! They play the numbers and they don't care who gets lost in the shuffle. They wrangle and finagle the system to their advantage and to suck the most money out of the average homeowner. They screwed so many people and it came back to bite them.

> You can take advantage of the current situation and make a fortune off of foreclosures.

Federal banks have power because they are protected by the federal government. Did you know that any federal bank can locate its main charter office in a state with high usury interest rates (like South Dakota and Delaware) and charge those high rates in ANY state, even states that have interest caps? They play the system to be able to squeeze the most out of you.

And squeeze they do.

Squeeze game

This issue came up in a lawsuit, *Watters vs Wachovia*, which was decided by the Supreme Court in April 2007. In essence, the decision in this case allowed federal regulators to be the big bad guys and stomp down any efforts that individual states make or try to make to regulate mortgage lenders.

And of course, there is not any real federal regulation in place, nor did the Supreme Court institute any. The states are stuck and the feds get their way.

Which brings to mind the ugly monsters of universal default and double-cycle billing that have been the industry standards for years while the feds look the other way.

Do you remember my ranting on universal default? You have paid your bill on time every month in full to one creditor, but if you miss a payment to another creditor, a different separate creditor, the notion of universal default means that the first creditor can rack up your interest rate and charge you more!

Give me a break!

Why should the first creditor even know what you are doing with the other creditors, first of all, and it should not matter one iota what you do with other creditors. As long as you pay Creditor #1 every month, he should not be able to up your rate because of what you do with Creditor #2. But so it goes.

Endless games

And the feds don't blink when the creditors bill you and charge interest on money that was repaid. My blood pressure is rising as I type. Maybe lately, since the mortgage debacle, there have been talks and minimal efforts and long coffee conversations about regulations being needed, but the lobbyists are still around and as powerful as ever.

They don't give up easily. Neither do I.

It was not all that long ago, when bankers were trusted fellows and deals were made with handshakes. Both parties were trusted and rarely did a home go into foreclosure. What has happened to our country?! Today, experts estimate that the greedy practices of the bankers and mortgage lenders siphoned off $9 billion in equity from homeowners! $9 BILLION!

If that number does not scream predatory lending, I don't know what does.

Power of the people

I am telling you that it is up to me and it is up to you. Write your Congressman/woman and tell them to get real and to get down to business. They have power. Tell them to use it and stop kowtowing to the lobbyists. Better yet, tell them to stop taking bribes from the lobbyists. Oh, they say it's not a bribe, but wining, dining, gifts, yachting parties, private jet lunches, and whatever else goes on is not standard business protocol in your world, is it? What they do is, in my opinion, a bribe. "I do this for you, and you, Mr. Congressman, do this for me."

Same old song and dance.

The so-called regulatory agencies, the Federal Reserve Board and the Office of the Comptroller of Currency, are basically there to maintain the stability of banks. Their job is not really the protection of consumers. Who do you think should be protecting you, the consumer? Yep, your elected officials in Washington. You elected them. They work for you. They seem to have forgotten that.

Argh ...

It is a tangled system. The loopholes exist and the feds need to close them. In 2006, when the whole housing crisis was beginning, over 50% of mortgages were with mortgage lending companies like mortgage brokers and finance companies. They are not subject to bank regulations.

Well, again, gimme a break! If the greedy guys want to create new companies to circumvent rules—and we are still waiting for real rules on the banks—the feds need to step up to the plate. It should not matter what type of agency gives the loan. It should only matter that the loan is a mortgage, and all mortgages should be subject to certain regulations that protect the citizen taking out that loan.

Plain and simple. No brainer to me.

> ...all mortgages should be subject to certain regulations that protect the citizen...

It can be likened to the tax on cigarettes. There is a tax, no matter where you buy them. How about if we say, okay, you who buy your cigs in the grocery store in Texas don't have to have any tax or age restrictions, but you who buy at the gas station in Ohio do.

That doesn't make any sense. Same with mortgages. If you take out a loan to buy a house, there should be nationwide protections for you, no matter who gives you that loan. Is that so hard? Hello, Washington, are you listening?

Frustration ...

Excuse me, while I vent some more! The greed that has taken over our country is hard to take. We were all shocked by the Enron scandal a few years back and couldn't fathom how anyone could be such a greedy SOB. Now the news stories are never ending with reports of greedy SOBs.

The New York Attorney General started digging the dirt on the top dog at Merrill Lynch, John Thain. This guy takes the cake. Or actually, he takes whatever he can get.

Besides the huge losses at Merrill Lynch—the huge losses that Thain as CEO failed to disclose—he tried to take a monster bonus for himself.

When the reality of the extent of the loss became known—$15 billion, that is not small potatoes—he went off on a ski trip. Hey, so what if the company he was in charge of was tanking; he had to hit the slopes. A greedy SOB has his priorities after all.

Get this—this dude spent $1.2 million of shareholder money redecorating his office. Some people have no shame. His list of little expenditures include:

$87,000 for an area rug
$15,000 for a sofa
$28,000 on curtains

This is the kind of executive we do not need in America. Sadly, there are way too many of them.

I have ranted and digressed down that tangent long enough. We must get back to the original topic, foreclosures.

OPM

While I am on the subject of houses and money and ways to get money, let's talk about a concept called OPM, Other People's Money. You may think I am crazy when I say you can buy a foreclosure property, or any property, for that matter. I am not crazy.

You can buy property or assets no matter what your financial situation is, no matter what your credit score is, no matter how much cash you have in the bank. You can start working your way into wealth with no cash outlay of your own. Using Other People's Money is brilliant and you can do it too.

Example of Other People's Money

Let's use Sally as an example. Sally had awful credit, but did not let that stop her. She knew OPM, Other People's Money, was her ticket to ride. It may seem like a new concept to you, but I am here to tell you: You can do almost anything and not spend a dime or a dollar of your own.

Other People's Money is one of the best kept secrets of success. And now the secret is yours.

No money from you

Here is one story: Sally found a rental property that she wanted to invest in. The seller agreed to carry the financing. Her poor credit was not an issue in getting a loan because the seller was playing the part of the bank. Her loan was with him. He knew that she could afford the monthly payment and they reached an agreement.

Sally and the seller entered into a contract for the property. The seller then partnered back with her, keeping 50% ownership for himself. So even with lousy credit, Sally became 50% owner of an investment rental property. Pretty cool, huh?

How did this happen? She became the manager of the properties as well. That was part of the deal. Sally gladly took on the responsibility of property manager.

After two years of managing the properties, Sandy then sold back two units to the seller, and she kept one in her ownership. Sally made $80,000 on the deal! $80,000 in two years is a good return on investment for her, wouldn't you say? That is a nice sum for someone who had a very bleak credit score. That is a nice sum for anyone.

Why not?

You may be asking yourself, why would the seller finance the deal? Why not? Why would the seller do anything? There are hundreds of unique reasons why people do what they do. In this case, Sally agreed to be property manager.

You never know until you ask. The magic words of "Will you finance this deal?" or "Can you carry the contract?" may start new deals that even the seller had not thought of at first. Do not be afraid to ask if there is anything the seller is willing to do to make the deal happen and be a good transaction for both of you.

In this case, the seller financed the deal and retained 50% ownership. It was a good deal for him. He had Sandy to take over half of the financial burden, which lightened his load financially, and she managed the rental properties, which freed him up to do other things with his time.

You never know when someone needs some cash and will carry the contract themselves. Maybe they don't even need the cash, but can see the benefit to both of you. Who knows what can happen. If you think that OPM is not going to happen for you, think again.

There are opportunities all around you, once you start looking for them.

Other People's Money—it comes in unexpected places and in unexpected ways. Once you grasp the idea, and start asking, you'll be pleasantly surprised at the deals you can make—even if you have no money or no credit.

Even while you are still in the process of ridding yourself of debt, you can move forward. These kinds of ventures are great avenues to building wealth. Like I have said a million times, for a million reasons, you never know until you ask.

Helpful hints

No matter if you are buying a foreclosure to turn around and sell, a house for your own use, or a rental property, you need to know a few basics. Bob Allen is a real estate expert and I have learned a lot from him. Some advice I have gleaned I would like to share with you.

A little preparation is the key to the success. An ounce of prevention is worth a pound of dollar bills. People who are new to the real estate investment world make a lot of the same mistakes. You don't have to.

Follow three simple tips for starters:

✔ Do not buy a property without inspecting it.
✔ Do not pay more than what it is worth (especially now!).
✔ Do not buy a property without researching the title.

Those tips seem like common sense, but many people do not take the time to follow through on those three items.

Learn the lingo

If you are entering the world of foreclosures, be ready to learn the terms that are used. Ever heard of junior liens or senior liens? Liens are basically the mortgages on the property. The senior lien is the first mortgage and the one with the most clout. That is the one you want. A mistake people make is that they buy a junior lien and not a senior lien.

The guy holding the senior lien is the guy with the trump cards. If you do not do a title search and buy a junior lien, you could be out the entire amount that you paid. Ouch, that would hurt. So take the time to follow the three steps above.

Do not buy a property without seeing it with your own eyes. A picture may paint a thousand words, but one home inspection is worth a million more. Research the market and do not overpay. Do not pay more for a foreclosure or any property. You also need to be smart and have the title work run. That way you know if there is more than one lien on a property and if there are any issues. You want a clean title.

And if you are buying a foreclosure, or any property that you plan to turn around and sell for a profit, you need to make sure to pay the taxes and the insurance on the property during the time you own it.

Finding foreclosures

There are several kinds of properties that you can find at a good price. You can ask your local bank for a list. They are more than willing to unload. Some government agencies, as well as the banks, have foreclosed properties.

✔ HUD or VA defaulted loan properties
✔ Fannie Mae and Freddie Mac defaulted loan properties
✔ Default on taxes properties
✔ Law enforcement seized properties

I already made it clear that you need to inspect a property before you buy it. Pictures on flyers or websites can be misleading.

You may hear ads on the radio or TV, or see sites on the internet, that advertise thousands of homes for sale. It has been my understanding that those lists are not always accurate. They are simply trying to make a buck and sell you a list. You can make your own list. You can do a little research and find plenty of properties on your own.

> Some government agencies, as well as the banks, have foreclosed properties.

Find some people

Don't be intimidated if this is new to you. You need knowledgeable people to help you with foreclosures and real estate transactions. Ask your friends and family. Find a trusted home inspector, real estate agent, a real estate attorney, an accountant, and a title company expert. If you are not a handyman, get someone who is or hire a contractor. They can give you an idea of how much repairs will cost before you make the commitment to buy the rental property or foreclosed home.

You can rely on the expertise of others and it can make the whole process much smoother, and in the end, more profitable.

Finding properties

There are many foreclosures on the market these days. You can simply drive around various neighborhoods in your town and see for sale signs or auction signs. Word of mouth is always a great way of learning what is out there. If you tell people that you are looking for foreclosed properties, you may be surprised at how many are available.

Other places to look/people to ask:
- ✔ Attorneys
- ✔ Real estate agents
- ✔ Banks or mortgage companies
- ✔ Foreclosure websites
- ✔ Public record of divorce decrees
- ✔ Foreclosure and bankruptcy notices in local paper
- ✔ Everyone you know

A few basic tips

As with any real estate transaction, you need to keep your emotions out of the deal. Keep your poker face, even if you are excited about the deal. After you inspect the property, you (and your helpful experts) can estimate what you should offer.

Don't get into bidding wars. Whatever is your top bid, commit to that price and do not go over it. You want to make a good return on your investments. You want to maximize your profits.

Possession issues

We've all heard that possession is nine-tenths of the law. Yep. There are times when you buy a foreclosed property, you can take possession right away. There are also many times that the homeowner can take up to a year to vacate the property. Even after the time period is up, there are times when the homeowner has to be evicted. It can be messy. Maybe you only want to buy a property that is empty. It is up to you, but something to be aware of.

Do the quick "flip"

Many times properties are bought, you do a little repair and updating, and then you turn around and sell it. The quicker the turnaround time the better. The longer you hang on to the property, the longer you pay the insurance and taxes, plus now you have to pay utilities.

The idea is to have your remodel work planned out even before you buy the property. That way, work can begin as soon as you get possession. You also have to follow all the old rules of real estate. Location matters. And you don't want to be the nicest house on the block. To get a good price, you must price right for the neighborhood.

Sell it quick

A real estate agent can help you set a good sales price when you are ready to sell. You want a profit, but you also want a quick sale. Do not price yourself too high. You don't want this house to sit on the market for long. And you do not want to have to mess with reducing the sales price. Set it right at first and you will get a quick sale.

Some people think they can make a larger profit by doing the sale themselves. In general, this is not true. Homes sell quicker and with a better price when selling with a creative real estate agent.

You need to find a real estate agent who understands how to sell during a tough market. Interview ten agents before you select someone to work with. Trust me, there will be plenty of agents to talk to. This is a "hungry" time for them. But only work with an agent who has a strong track record of sales experience through various real estate cycles. Let them show you their portfolio of properties they've sold lately.

Before you list with an agent, try to negotiate the best real estate fee. Generally, the fees nationwide are about 6% of the eventual sales price. The lower the commission, the more profit in your pocket. Realtors don't like to "cut their commissions." But if you're up front about your desire to keep fees low, your realtor might accommodate you.

What is my motto? JUST ASK! It doesn't cost you anything to ask. "Would you consider a 4% fee (or 3%) instead of the usual 6%?" If they say, "yes," you just saved yourself potentially thousands of dollars.

> ...try to negotiate the best real estate fee.

If they say no to a lower commission, then ask, "Is that the best you can do?" They might be willing to provide some money for closing, a free appraisal, or a lower commission on a future purchase or sale. If they know you are doing more transactions, they should be smart and be willing to work with you.

If the agent is not willing to give you extra goodies or a lower fee, you have a ton of other real estate agents to work with. Just make sure that the one you choose has a proven track record.

Talk it up

Start talking about selling it as soon you buy it. Let the word spread that as soon as you fix it up, it will be on the market. A buyer may come to you before you even list it. This happens more than you would think.

The basic rule of real estate: make sure the house has curb appeal. Clean up the yard and clean the whole house. Little things matter.

Have a clean, welcoming front door. As soon as the For Sale sign goes up, you want to start getting calls.

A primer on the foreclosure process

There are four stages of the foreclosure process. You can make money in any one of them. Again, I defer to the experts, like Robert Allen, for the nitty gritty here. You will be glad to learn from the top dogs.

The first stage is the pre-foreclosure period. This is when the owner of the home has missed a payment or two and knows that he or she is in trouble. They, the homeowners, are very willing during this period because the fear of foreclosure looms over them. This is an ideal time to help them save their credit rating by taking over their payments.

However, it's not easy to find people who are in this situation because there is no public record of the late payment activity (and the bank won't tell you). The homeowner may have received a letter from the bank informing them of their late status, but no notice of default has been filed at the county court house. You will have to rely on word of mouth, but never, ever, underestimate the power of word of mouth.

Pre-foreclosure

Sometimes the best way to find a pre-foreclosure is by passing out your business card to everyone you meet. On the back of your business card, offer a "finder's fee" to anyone (or anyone they might know) who points you in the direction of a great real estate opportunity.

The amount of the fee you are willing to pay can be from $100 cash to $1,000 or more. It depends upon how good the deal is. You can also run small ads in local newspapers to attract potential sellers. The small investment you make in finding the properties can pay you back in a big way.

Notice of default

The second stage of the foreclosure process is after the notice of default has been filed at the county court house. Then, it becomes public knowledge and everyone knows the homeowners are late in their payments.

This is when the clock starts to run. In most states, the foreclosure timeframe is 90 days. If the payments have not been brought current during this time, the home could be sold to the highest cash bidder.

For those who buy the lists of homes in foreclosure, those lists are compiled from these public records. There is a chance that a letter you send to people whose homes are in foreclosure can generate good results for you. After all, you only need one good response in a thousand letters to yield a nice profit. It may cost you about $500 in mailing costs to mail a bunch of letters, but if someone agreed to sell to you, and you make a nice profit, that $500 was a good investment. It is totally up to you if you want to go that route.

Of course, many people going through foreclosure these days are "underwater" in their mortgage. They owe more than the value of their property. A property may have a mortgage of $300,000 but is now only worth $250,000.

There are a lot of these situations and these are not the type of deals that you want. You want to buy a property in foreclosure whose mortgage is substantially below the value of the property. For example, you want to buy a home worth $300,000 for only $200,000.

You want to be able to pay off the seller and bring the payments current to stop the foreclosure.

Auction

The third stage of the foreclosure process is the day of the sale when the property is sold at auction. If you are doing foreclosure research and found a home with a loan balance of $200,000 and a value of $300,000, you would want to contact the homeowner before the sale to the public.

Round up your posse of experts and dig up some cash and make the deal. When you show your friends and family how much profit you can make, you should be able to get a little help from these new investors.

You can stop the foreclosure and turn an incredible profit. The property, even in a down market, could sell quickly if you make sure you price it the first time at the right price. Do not get greedy.

After the sale

The final stage of the foreclosure process is after the foreclosure sale. The vast majority of foreclosed homes go directly back to the bank. The banks have foreclosed on so many homes now. They do not want all these homes. That is not how they make money.

Many times, in fact most of the time, the banks are willing to sell the property for less than they've got in it, often thousands of dollars less. The real estate gurus predict that there will be hundreds of thousands of homes resold by the foreclosing bank at prices that are substantially less than the cost of the original mortgage.

The money part

Okay, I hear you. You are saying that this information is all great, but you don't have any money to put down or to buy a cheap foreclosure house. If at all possible, cut a deal and use some OPM! Other People's Money is always an option to pursue. Even if you are in foreclosure yourself!

Your credit report or your own lack of cash need not hold you back. Maybe you have a co-signor; maybe you have an investor. Whatever you do, make sure you have enough financing to make it a cash deal. Cash is what seals the deal. Don't worry. We have a chapter on how to get cash quick!

Some tips to get you in the foreclosure frame of mind:

- ✔ Go to several foreclosure auctions ahead of time so you know what happens. You want to know the actual process of how to bid and what kind of paperwork they will need from you when you are ready to buy.

- ✔ Search the listings in your area. Talk to people. When you find a property that you want, follow it every week in the listings.

- ✔ Inspect the property yourself and take pictures.

- ✔ Find out what other homes in the area have sold for recently.

- ✔ Have the title work done.

- ✔ Talk to the attorney for the foreclosed property several days before the date of the auction to make sure that the auction will be held and if there is a minimum bid.

- ✔ Visit the property again right before the auction starts to make sure nothing has changed since you first toured it.

- ✔ Before the auction, go to your bank for a cashier's check.

- ✔ The goal is 20% return on investment. Figure out what your maximum bid must be to keep this profit margin. Know that maximum number and don't go over it.

- ✔ If you do indeed win the bidding process, congratulations!

- ✔ Get insurance, record the deed, and pay off the bid amount.

- ✔ Make contact with the homeowners to help ensure a smooth transition.

- ✔ Establish a working relationship with the homeowners so they will move and not force an eviction.

Online help

Visit www.homebuyerfunds.com, a resource for both homeowners and the ones wanting to buy. This site is a database of *"Free Homebuyer Grants & Home Repair Grants From Government & Private Agencies."*

The site is free information, which is always a good thing. They claim "an extensive, searchable database of thousands of funds for current and prospective homeowners who want to purchase or repair their homes offered by the government, non-profit agencies, and private organizations."

If you need financial help with home improvements, check it out. If you need help with buying a home, give it a click. If you need help trying to avoid the foreclosure process, take a look.

> ...a resource for both homeowners and the ones wanting to buy.

Homebuyerfunds.com has a free online certification course for homebuyer education that satisfies HUD requirements for housing assistance programs. There is also a free search tool for homebuyer assistance programs and for home repair and improvement assistance programs too.

Check out the feature Apply For Funding Now. You enter your state, your credit profile (excellent; good; fair; needs improvement; or poor), the type of property (single family; multifamily; condo; townhome; mobile home; or manufactured home), and type of loan (home purchase; home refinance; home equity; or debt consolidation), and click on the SUBMIT button.

You will be directed to other sites for an appropriate quote and information on how to find the best loan for your needs. You can print a home loan checklist, calculate payments, and get tips and advice on a wide range of topics from "Finding a bad credit mortgage" to "Refinance tips" to "What is PMI?"

The information is endless; it's helpful when buying property and it is useful when cleaning up your credit as well.

I know this chapter went long. Too much information? I don't think so. Use this as a reference guide! You'll be glad that you are armed with all this advice!

Check with a realtor or bank right now and you will be amazed at the deals out there. Go to zillow.com or realtor.com or foreclosure. com for foreclosure homes that are available now for just hundreds of dollars.

CHAPTER 19

Make Money From Your Home

"My home…It is my retreat and resting place from wars, I try to keep this corner as a haven against the tempest outside, as I do another corner in my soul."
~Michel de Montaigne

This chapter title can be interpreted in two ways. You can make money working from your home. And we'll get to that. You also can get money from changing the way you pay for your home.

Most people who are homeowners would love to pay off their home faster. How about you? Do you fall into that category?

Let's talk about the average person.

The usual

With a traditional thirty-year mortgage, a homeowner ends up paying about double the purchase price of the home after those thirty years of interest have been paid. Yeah. Double. That is a boatload of cash.

With a very simple method, you can pay less interest, and thus pay less on the very same mortgage. Same house, paid off quicker. Sound appealing?

Pay Weekly or Biweekly

One money-saving tip is simple and obvious, yet most people don't do it because they are creatures of habit and it can be hard to teach an old dog a new trick.

Mortgages are usually set up as a monthly payment. Let's say your mortgage is $1,000 per month. Due on the first of the month, you pay the full $1,000 and wait until next month to roll around, and you pay again. You can knock off tremendous interest expense by paying early. The way interest calculations are made, prepaying has a huge impact. One easy way to pay early is to pay weekly.

The amount of your payment does not change; the same amount of money leaves your checkbook. You simply pay installments each week, so that by the first of the month, you have paid the entire amount due in full. In our example of $1,000, you would pay $250 each week. Your monthly expense is not changed at all, your budget is the same. All you do is change the timing of your payments.

Save thousands

It can save you literally thousands of dollars over the life of the mortgage! And this method of prepayments takes off years from the mortgage, too. You can cut the life of your 30-year mortgage by many years just by paying each week!

For those who get paid every week, this can be an easy switch to make. If you get paid every two weeks, you can do this prepayment method as well. Biweekly payments of $500 can be made.

The way the interest calculations are run, the prepayment amounts knock off some principal and the interest is thus compounding on a smaller balance. Less interest over the years and less years to pay. Win-win.

This also means more equity built up faster.

"Bonus" payments

There are other simple ways to get your home paid off quicker. Even if you make just one extra mortgage payment each year, you can take as much as three years off the life of your loan. Some people make lump sum "bonus" payments against principal whenever they come into a little money, any time of year, in any amount, as often as they like. Paying down the debt decreases the amount of interest that needs to be rung up. Even as little as $15 every two weeks applied to your mortgage can cut one and a half years off.

> Make sure that your mortgage allows the prepayment option.

Any change in your spending habits can be applied against the mortgage. Make sure that your mortgage allows the prepayment option. Most do, but be wise and double check before you follow this line of attack.

An example

Let's look at Gilligan and Skipper. In this example, we'll say Gilligan has tackled the task of improving his credit report and now has a credit score of 720. He qualifies for an interest rate of 5.5%.

Skipper has been lying around watching reruns on television and waiting for a magic fairy to come hand him a winning lottery ticket. Skipper's FICO score was 550, and the mortgage company gave him an interest rate of 9.3%.

They both took out $200,000 mortgages.

Gilligan will have a monthly mortgage payment of $1,100. Skipper will have a monthly payment of around $1,650. Skipper will pay and pay and pay. He pays over $500 more each and every month. After a year that means he shelled out $6,600 more than Gilligan.

If they both pay for thirty years, Skipper will pay $186,000 more in interest. That is nearly what the original mortgage amount was.

Let's say Skipper wised up. He decided to pay off his mortgage early. He took his monthly amount due of $1,650 and paid weekly installments of about $415, making sure that the full amount was paid by the first of every month.

This one small tactic saved him thousands of dollars and years off the time to pay. A very wise move, indeed.

Refinancing with PMI

Let's use an example of Larry. He bought his first house with less than 20% down, which meant the bank charged him PMI, Private Mortgage Insurance. PMI is a fee that the lenders collect until you, the homebuyer, have 20% equity in your home.

It's a gimmick, a ripoff, a way for them to siphon more money out of you. Make sure that when you reach 20%, you contact the lender to remove this fee as they may or may not automatically do so. It is up to you to pay attention.

PMI is money out the window. You don't want to pay it any longer than you have to. Better yet, if you are buying a home, find a way to make a 20% down payment so you do not have to pay PMI.

In our example, Larry also had a less than great credit score so his interest rate was 9%. He felt powerless and accepted his fate, not realizing he had it within himself to make things happen for the better.

Then Larry got a hold of *Debt Cures*. He read both books and Larry took action. He cleaned up his credit report and improved his credit score and went back to his banker. Larry refinanced his mortgage for a much better rate and saved thousands of dollars. He had over 20% equity now, so he stopped paying the PMI, too.

Think about it

Refinancing can be a great way to reduce your payment and your overall interest expense. Usually there is a fee to refinance your mortgage. Whatever the closing costs are can be divided by your monthly savings (your old payment amount compared to the new monthly payment after the re-fi) to determine how long it will take you to recover the fees associated with refinancing.

If you are going to be in your house a few years, it usually is cost beneficial to do the refinance. Run the numbers yourself before you refinance, but in most cases, it's a great strategy for an immediate payment reduction and overall long-term savings.

That's a win-win. More money from your house means more money to pay off other debt.

Mortgage renegotiation

Times are tough. Yeah, we know.

If you are among the many needing help with the mortgage payment, you are not alone. Set the stage. Average Annie struggled for months trying to pay the house payment, but her circumstances kept snowballing and the payments became just too much to bear. After everything she did to try to keep her house, she felt she had no choice but to face foreclosure.

Bye, bye, dream home. So long American Dream.

Is this anything like your story?

How about Average Sam. He had a mortgage balance of $190,000 when the bank foreclosed on his house. Because the market tanked, the bank was only able to sell Sam's house for $150,000. That leaves $40,000 not paid on the mortgage. The bank "relieved" the debt because there was no way to collect from Sam or get more on the sale. The $40,000 is called forgiveness of debt.

Lost

Whatever Sam paid in all those years on his house is lost to him; it's money out the window. He has no equity and he has no house. The bank took his house and he has nothing to show for all the payments he did make.

> He has no equity and he has no house.

AND the forgiveness of debt by the bank is considered taxable income in the eyes of the IRS. That means Average Sam has to report $40,000 of income on his tax return. There was no tax withheld because he did not receive any actual cash, and come year end, he will be liable for taxes on that amount.

Double whammy.

Sum it up. Average Sam had no funds to pay his mortgage, causing him to lose his home. Now he has no funds to pay taxes on an additional invisible $40,000. It's quite a catch. Take someone in hardship and make it even harder.

Talk about kicking a man when he's down.

New law

Because so many people were in this situation, a new tax law was passed at the end of 2007. An unpaid mortgage balance, up to $2 million, is now excluded from taxable income. The amount of debt relieved or forgiven, up to $2 million, is no longer the death blow.

Under the new law, Average Sam would NOT have to claim the $40,000 as income, and would NOT have to pay taxes on it.

That is a new law that I can support. I can't say that every day.

But didn't I start out this section on mortgage renegotiation? Instead of going into foreclosure, try to modify your mortgage or renegotiate the terms.

How it works

The bank restructures the mortgage to give different terms and a payment that the homeowner can afford. It is common sense. Something they should have been doing all along instead of all the foreclosures.

By renegotiating and getting a lower monthly payment, Average Sam would be able to stay in his house, and the bank would still be getting regular payments. Makes a good thing for both ends of the deal.

When the whole mortgage meltdown crisis started, banks were in foreclosure mode and didn't work with their homeowners. As the crazy crisis continued and the mortgage lenders were taking on too many homes in foreclosure and getting stuck with them, the idea of mortgage renegotiation became more appealing.

The banks have learned that taking back your house means they have to pay the taxes and the insurance, and wait for it to sell. Months and months of this made them open their eyes. Keeping you in the house, with a lesser payment, means income to them and you do not have to lose your house. It's a win-win.

Duh.

Don't be shy

People in all parts of the country, of all races, of all income levels, and of all education levels are now seeking mortgage renegotiation. It can be your ticket to keeping your house. ONE MILLION mortgages have been renegotiated since this whole debacle began.

I consider mortgage renegotiation another set of magic words.

People are getting house payments that are 40% lower than what they paid before. Some are getting 60% lower. By getting a payment that you can afford, you will not mess up your credit report.

The renegotiation itself does not get reported. All it means for you is that you have a payment that you are able to make so no late payments appear on the credit record. You are able to keep your house and keep your credit score intact.

With a renegotiation, it is your same mortgage so there are no fees involved like with a refinance.

Cali

The state of California blazed the trail for mortgage modifications. The California state attorney filed charges against Countrywide, stating that their *"lending practices turned the American dream into a nightmare for tens of thousands of families by putting them into loans they couldn't understand and ultimately couldn't afford."*

Yep. Countrywide and a whole lot of other mortgage lenders too.

Countrywide is practicing restitution in a way by contacting homeowners—400,000 of them—and working out new loan terms with them so they do not go into default.

Caution

As with any crisis or trend, there are the guys out to make a profit off your trouble. Beware the credit counselor who wants to charge you to renegotiate for you.

First of all, this is something you can do yourself. You don't need some scamster to make off with your money, be it $500 or $5,000. If you do want advice, there are non-profit agencies who will help for little or no cost.

In a nutshell, you have to go to your mortgage lender and request new terms because you are unable to pay the current monthly payment. You have to be able to show that with your income, you will be able to make the modified payment.

Do it

What the mortgage lender does is modify your current terms. Maybe you get a lower interest rate for a set amount of time. Maybe you get a lower payment and the length of the loan gets extended.

Usually it is temporary, but some modifications remain for the life of the loan.

Some loans get a lower rate, for example from 8% down to 6%, for the next five years. That reduction in interest rate makes a nice reduction in your payment.

Some loans get spread out over a longer time. Instead of a 30-year mortgage, lenders are doing 40-year loan terms now. A 40-year loan at 5% is a nicely reduced lower payment and free money in your bank account every month.

According to CNN, in February 2009, nearly 250,000 homeowners received either mortgage modifications or repayment plans from their lenders.

What's the diff?

In case you are wondering about the difference between refinance and modification: Refinance is paying off the old loan by opening a brand new loan. It requires a new closing and paperwork, etc. Loan modification is making changes to your current existing loan to make it more manageable.

As long as you have a job, the odds for modifying your loan are in your favor. The federal government passed a new bill in March 2009 for the hurting homeowners. The Making Home Affordable Program, according to the *LA Times*, "provides $75 billion in financial incentives to lenders so that they will reduce interest payments."

> As long as you have a job, the odds for modifying your loan are in your favor.

In some cases the program allows for a reduction in principal so that the monthly payment will not exceed 31% of the borrower's income, but that reduction is only temporary. The set-aside portion of the principal will have to be repaid when the loan is paid off or refinanced or the house is sold.

"It's for homeowners who 'have experienced a significant change in income or expenses to the point that the current mortgage payment is no longer affordable,' according to program guidelines."

(Source: www.latimes.com/business/la-fi-cover22-2009mar22,0,7096135. story?page=2)

If you think you want to modify your loan, first talk to a mortgage counselor at your local HUD office. Their services are FREE. Find the local office at www.hud.gov. The counselor will review your income and your current mortgage and be able to determine if you are a candidate for a loan modification.

Many loan modifications are done by extending the life of the loan. Same mortgage amount spread over a longer number of years means a lower payment for you. Some modifications are a temporary reduction in the interest rate which again lowers your monthly payment. The bank or the counselor can guide you in how your loan can be modified.

The sticking point with modifications is that you must be able to pay the new reduced payment. Your current income needs to be able to support making a payment, just not the current payment that you are unable to handle.

With a reduced payment, you will escape the burden of "too much mortgage." The ability to make the monthly payment will lighten your load and ease your mind. That is what these debt cures are all about.

CHAPTER 20

Make Money From Home: Part 2

"What is more agreeable than one's home?"
~Marcus Tullius Cicero

Besides paying less for your home, you can make money from home. No matter what your debt is, you can make money right here, right now, and you can make it from your own home. Yes, you can.

A home-based business is a great idea, in any economy, in any era.

No more door to door

Do you have visions of lugging boxes in your car? You don't have to go door-to-door anymore like the old encyclopedia salesman and you don't have to call people on the phone. There are hundreds of opportunities to make money from your home and all you need is the internet.

Before I get ahead of myself (I do that a lot), review the chapter on "10K in a day" or whatever we called it for ways to make money fast. If you think you want a little start-up cash and don't know where it will come from, refresh your memory and flip back a few pages.

Once you get revved up, the ideas start flowing. Creativity takes over and you have many ways to make a buck. I have thought up a few more.

1. **Sell Some Assets.** Do you have a time share or a vacation home that you never use? Sell it! There is no sense paying the annual maintenance on something you are not enjoying. Somebody will LOVE to take it off your hands!

2. **Rent Your Assets.** Not sure if you want to sell that time share condo or vacation home on the lake? Rent it out! You can still have use of it when you want it, and you can collect big bucks from others who will be able to enjoy it too. Win-win, and cash to you.

3. **America's Got Talent and so do YOU.** Are you a handyman? Can you paint the walls? Pound a nail? People NEED you! You can spend a weekend taking care of little household jobs for one person and be "rich" by Monday! Charge by the project or the hour—doesn't matter. Big bucks are waiting!

Be creative. Be bold. Sell yourself. (Just wanted to make sure you were still reading.) Don't overlook the obvious. I know people who have yard sales every summer and make at least a grand. They get rid of kids' toys and clothes, making room in the closets and making a bundle of dough in the process. Maybe you have a service you can offer that is worth "gold."

Do you enjoy dog sitting? House sitting? Baby sitting? You may not make $5K in a day, but it is astonishing how much money you can make simply doing things you enjoy. Do you like gardening? Take care of the flowers and plants of your neighbors for cash. See what I mean? The possibilities are endless.

I know someone who makes and sells decorated cakes and makes great money at it. Same for another friend who makes specialty cookies. I also know someone who is a personal chef for others and makes nice money. There is a person in Los Angeles who personalizes clothing, blankets, and similar items. She is able to now support her entire family—a husband and FIVE kids!—from this gig!

Doing what you love can bring you FAST CASH! And it can become FAT CASH!

There are dozens and dozens of ways to get money fast. Use this as a guide to get your creative juices flowing and see what ideas you come up with. Each one of these ideas will get you some bucks, and some will get you a whole lotta bucks.

Now and longer

These ideas that I give you are multipurpose. Yes, I realize that you are looking for ways to make money virtually overnight to get out of debt and out of the pit of bills, bills, bills. That is what I am here for, to help you dig out and cure your debt.

> You can be cured of your debt from here on out.

That is part two of my purpose. Cure your debt. Cure it, not band-aid it or patch it up as a temporary fix. A cure is forever.

You can be cured of your debt from here on out. Seriously.

Using the tactics we cover in these pages, you can pay it off because you can reduce what you owe. You can get your credit score and credit report whipped into shape and that means lower bills. You can change the way you pay for your house. You can make money off a foreclosed home. You can do a lot of things.

It all works together to get you out of the current muck and mired down situation and on to easier times.

Dream it, believe it

And what you learn, you apply and practice from now until eternity. These ideas of how to make fast cash can turn into a business that you never dreamed of, and money that you never dreamed possible.

Times are tough but you are tougher

Things happen when times are tough. People take chances and think in new ways. Now is your time.

I just read a story of a hairdresser who got laid off. Yeah, every industry is hurting and no one is exempt from the pink slip. This gal didn't just go cry and pout. She heard from a friend that the elderly population cannot get out to the beauty salon but want their hair done. This laid-off lady took her scissors and shampoo and started making house calls.

She found a whole new business opportunity and makes even more money than she did when she was a regular stylist at the mall. Just because you keep hearing "times are tough" does not mean that opportunity does not exist.

Your skills are needed

People like you, and whatever your special skills you may have, are needed, more than ever. If you get anything from my books, I hope it is the message to never, ever give up. I have faced adversity and trouble and opposition and a helluva lot of ugly stuff. I didn't give up. And now, through it all, I can call myself a success story.

I believe you can too.

Right now, you feel that you are in a pinch. You are in a bind to pay off the bills. I understand. Use these ideas to make the cash you need. Once you get out of panic mode, you can start to think about your future.

What works for you? What do you enjoy doing?

Are you one of the cake bakers? You can do it for fun and profit. Every success story started as a small story. Mrs. Fields' Cookies, the Auntie Em Pretzels, every ice cream or juice guy or whatever. They started out of necessity or just for fun, and the business exploded into a full-blown big deal.

Be a success story

Do you have secret aspirations of having your own company? Go for it. Now really is the time. The world needs entrepreneurs.

You can't sit around and wait to get hired at some old job when the economy is down. Jobs are scarce. Opportunities are not. You can make it happen for yourself. And maybe you don't have grand plans for a huge business, but let's say you do enjoy taking care of animals, for example.

You can have a small home-based business and never take it beyond that. You don't have to be a Fortune 500 company. You can make nice money and do something you love. Take that little inkling of an idea and make it your home-based business.

Someone who loves dogs is always needed to walk the dog, babysit the dog, shampoo the dog, trim the dog, make gourmet organic health food biscuits for the dog…Let your imagination run wild. If you have an idea, you can create a money-making business around that one simple idea. Brainstorm and discuss with friends. See all of the possibilities that exist and pick which feels right.

Make up simple business cards, post flyers, make a simple website. Word of mouth works tremendously well and doesn't cost a dime. Believe me when I say the possibilities are endless. You do one job and the word spreads. Before you know it, you are so busy, you may have to turn down clients.

You can work from home and make a nice living. And most of all, you can enjoy it.

Another way

Earlier I mentioned the internet. It is the greatest tool of our era. Online is the way of the world and because we have the world wide web, we can take our dreams of business and money to a whole new level. Many businesses now could not have existed several years ago.

> The beauty of the internet is cost savings and time savings.

I love the web!

The beauty of the internet is cost savings and time savings. One of the best ways to make money and keep making money is to get involved in a home based business that uses the internet.

The mighty internet

Call it what you will, I know people are suspicious, but there are many internet marketing companies that are not pyramid schemes. They are legitimate ways to make money. There are many and I am not endorsing any or getting paid to mention any, but think about the products that you know and love.

If you use a product and stand by it, don't you want to tell other people about it? And if you can help them out by offering the benefits of such product, wouldn't you want to do that? And if you make money along the way in doing so, even better.

The experts in this field maintain that you pick a product for many reasons and the number one reason is that you are passionate about it. I know that to be true. In my blunt opinion, passion sells.

That is so, but you can't fake passion. If you merely pick a gizmo or gadget or whatever to be your thing because it is the latest and greatest hot item, there is no guarantee that it will make you any money.

The thing with internet marketing is that the product you choose to sell should be something you believe in and something that is consumable. That means your customers will run out of it and need to order more.

I know a guy who sells candles and does okay, and yes, candles technically run out. But people buy them more as a favor to him or as a fundraiser kind of thing for their kids' school, not because they need another smelly candle.

Product WOW

The successful people in this market are the ones who tried a nutrition supplement, for example. They were wowed by it. They totally fell head over heels in love with the stuff. Their kids stopped getting sick, the allergies cleared up, the overall health and well-being of the family improved. Maybe there was weight loss involved, but a general feeling of "Wow, this product is amazing" was the initial attention getter.

Because they fell in love with the product, they wanted to get it monthly at the cheapest rate so they became a distributor. Getting the cheapest price made sense and they knew it was the right product for them.

Then little by little, they started telling their friends and family about Product Wow. And little by little, more people tried it and liked it too. They started selling Product Wow to said friends and family. The next thing they knew, they had a little side business and money was coming in, and it was all quite effortless. The money became a wow factor too.

So then, the realization comes over them and they decide to put a little more time into this side business and it really takes off. Sitting at home on the computer or talking on the phone to friends and acquaintances, a business is born.

I ran out and need to buy more ...

Once you get your customers rolling, they can order online. They can refer other customers to you or become distributors themselves and you get a reward for being the one to introduce them to the company. You sit back and get nice monthly checks for doing nothing more than telling people about a product that you believe in.

I am not making this up. This is how it works.

It all starts with passion about a product and when it is a consumable product, the sky is the limit where profits are involved. Selling objects can be great, but it is not the same thing. A great lamp is a great lamp, but if it can last a lifetime, there are no repeat sales. The idea of these internet marketing companies is repeat business.

If the vitamin drink you enjoy every morning is nearing empty, you order more. So you want to get involved with a product that is something that gets used up. I know people who make great incomes by selling nutritional supplements, skin care items, make up and beauty products, and even greeting cards through an online distributor system.

Share your passion

I don't want to name names because I will omit some and make some folks upset with me, but I think you get the idea. If you swear by XYZ face wash and how it has improved your complexion and made you look twenty years younger, you are going to share that knowledge with your friends. If you can make money by sharing your passion about XYZ, why wouldn't you?

The real treat is that you keep making money long after the initial sale. The residual income that comes to you month after month is the golden nugget. Spend a little bit of time getting people interested, then you make the sale and then you do nothing and you keep making money.

Yeah, it's a beautiful thing.

On a plane, on a train ...

Think about the products that you love and use regularly. Become a distributor and turn on everyone you know to why you love it. Then tell everyone you meet. You can be sitting next to someone on an airplane and in the normal chit chat of conversation that takes place, you can make a new customer. That new customer might become a distributor too. The income potential is off the charts.

It's easy. It's fun. It's usually no inventory and very little up-front costs to you to get started. People order and get their stuff shipped directly to them. You can have customers all over the country and depending upon the product, all over the world.

This kind of selling and income that the internet has made possible is a glorious thing. Never before could you have an operation that was so easy. And never before could you make so much money by doing so little and also never having to leave home.

Home can be a haven. Especially when the mailman brings those checks every month. Or, being the tech world that we live in, the automatic deposit that shows up in your account each month is a little piece of heaven.

Promote yourself

For many people, promotion and marketing do not come easy or naturally. Whatever kind of business you have, you need to toot your own horn.

This one link will take to you to several sites that will help you do just that. Business owners soon learn that marketing is just something you have to do. Make it easy on yourself and pick up some tips now.

There is a wealth of info at www.ahbbo.com/marketing-business-articles.html.

Keep going

Everyone needs a little encouragement from time to time. The small business owner even more so. Even if you work from home alone, you can find support on the internet. Look at bloggers in your area of interest. Start a blog of your own if you want. It can be a great marketing tool and a way to connect with others. Take a look at www.ahbbo.com/ownrace.html.

Need help with writing a business plan? Check out www.ahbbo.com/busplan.html.

Interested in the top ten myths of running your own biz from home? www.ahbbo.com/top10.html.

How about a little money tip? www.ahbbo.com/money.html.

Wondering how to get started? www.ahbbo.com/howdoi.html and www.ahbbo.com/righthomebusiness.html and www.ahbbo.com/checkhbb.html.

Top 25

According to AllBusiness.com, the top 25 home based businesses are:

Yoga instructor, personal trainer, tutor, medical/legal transcription, business coach, consulting, medical claims billing, accounting, web design, senior care services, photography, home inspection, remodeling, interior design, catering or personal chef, wedding/event planner, gift baskets, personal shopper, concierge, jewelry, computers, cleaning, carpet cleaning, pet grooming, child care.

(www.allbusiness.com/specialty-businesses/home-based-business/3315-1.html)

This list is just the tip of the iceberg.

Don't limit yourself. Think outside the box. What do you like to do? What are your special skills?

You can devise a home-based business and make money and love it.

> You can devise a home-based business and make money and love it.

Bonus

Forming a company has a huge benefit. You can get more credit as a business owner than as an individual. Your credit scores are separate, you the individual and you the business.

It is easier than you think to form a business. You can form an LLC online at www.legalzoom.com. It's fast and simple and not expensive.

Why?

Why do you want to be a business? As a business you have access to a much larger line of credit. MUCH LARGER. You could qualify for a line of credit of a million bucks. I see it all the time.

The great thing about a line of credit is that it is there for you, ready and waiting. You use a little of it or a lot of it, you make the decision. It is not a loan with a set installment payment. It is a pot of gold waiting for you at the end of your rainbow.

In general, the interest rates are usually lower for corporate businesses too. Think of all the possibilities. Are you excited?

A cool million

Can you imagine having a million bucks at your disposal? With your corporate tax ID number, you are a separate entity with a whole new fresh credit record. It's a bold new landscape.

Yet another huge benefit to forming your own company is the tax breaks you get! You can deduct all your business expenses and these can be quite substantial. When you are a business owner, much of what you spend time on and spend money on is for your business. Those expenses can be written off!

Talk to your financial advisor about forming a corporation or LLC and get started today!

Pick one

I have listed many ideas regarding how to get started and pick a business, but only you know what is right for you. If you get a headache being around children, then a day care probably is not the best bet.

I know a gal who makes bowls and purses out of old vinyl record albums. I know a guy who makes lamps out of wine bottles. I know a husband and wife team who started a business helping other parents navigate the waters of college aid and scholarships.

Opportunities are all around. Pick yours.

Have fun

Making money is fun. Making money without having to leave home is more fun. Try it. I think you'll like it.

CHAPTER 21

Bankruptcy

"It's a long and winding road ..."
~The Beatles

Making money chapter ... straight into bankruptcy. Confusing? Seem out of order? Yes and no. Even while in bankruptcy, I know people who have made money. They climbed out of the pit at their lowest moment and went on to millionaire status. Cross my heart.

But bankruptcy is a loaded word for some people. That may be so, but it is a topic we need to address.

Most people have mixed emotions when it comes to bankruptcy. It does not have to be your only out. Most of the time, I say you can avoid it. But I also realize how common it is and that some of you may be thinking about it.

An article in the *USA Today* from March 2009 says it best:

Cash-strapped families are seeking bankruptcy protection at nearly the same rate and in the same manner as they did before the much-debated 2005 bankruptcy law reform, a trend critics say proves the reform was a failure.

Congress wrangled for eight years before passing a reform act aimed at curbing abuse and ending an alarming rise in bankruptcy filings. With the economy in tatters and personal fortunes often in even worse shape these days, the bankruptcy law is beginning to undergo scrutiny again.

(Source: www.usatoday.com/money/economy/2009-03-22-reform-filings-bankruptcy_N.htm)

If you are facing bankruptcy or have filed, don't despair. I know many a millionaire with a bankruptcy filing in their pasts. It is more common than you think.

Because of the 2005 reform in the bankruptcy laws, what was supposed to help has really hindered. It costs more, takes longer and is more difficult to file now. And of course, the reform is better for the banks than the person filing for bankruptcy.

There goes my gag reflex again.

No help

Some studies say that the bankruptcy reform actually fueled the foreclosure crisis too. People are really stuck between a rock and a hard place. I hear stories of people who have nothing and cannot even afford to file for bankruptcy.

What's wrong with our legislators?!

In 2005, there was a record two million bankruptcy filings. What a sad commentary at the state of our union. After the reform law passed, the number of filings went down because so many people rushed to do it before the changes went into place.

In 2008, bankruptcy filings were on the rise again. To the tune of 1.1 million. In 2009, the experts predict that another 1.4 million will file. Some even venture to guess that the number will be closer to 1.6 million. Yikes.

No shame

Easy for me to say, but it needs to be repeated. There is no shame in filing for bankruptcy. Listen to the folks who know:

"One of the primary purposes of the bankruptcy law is to provide a way to grant debt relief to the honest-but-overextended debtor, who through no fault of his own is burdened by more debt than he can pay," says Sam Gerdano, executive director of the American Bankruptcy Institute, an independent research and education organization.

(www.usatoday.com/money/economy/2009-03-22-reform-filings-bankruptcy_N.htm)

What's new

The new law makes it more of a pain to file for bankruptcy, especially for higher income folks. Those people have to pass a "means" test. They have to provide pages and pages of paperwork, from tax returns and pay stubs to other sources of income, plus a detailed listing of all expenses. Some people just don't have their records.

"One of the primary purposes of the bankruptcy law is to provide a way to grant debt relief to the honest-but-overextended debtor..."

The government wants people to not file Chapter 7, which excuses most of the debt, including credit card balances, and instead file Chapter 13, which makes you pay all your debts still, just over an extended period of time.

What stinks

The credit card companies cry because bankruptcy filings put a debt in their budget. They say bankruptcy issues made them lose $40 billion a year. So they wanted to up their fees to cover their losses. Talk about no shame.

And get this. The bankruptcy reform has helped the credit card industry. Now you tell me, who is in bed with whom? The credit card lobbyists have their pals in Washington make it harder for people to file bankruptcy. Not only do these people have to keep paying on their credit card bills and not get a clean slate, the credit card companies can keep racking them with fees and fees and fees!

The experts know it

This is what the experts at Card Trak, a credit card research firm, have to say:

> Since the reform passed, the credit card industry's profits have grown. It earned $19.9 billion from penalty fees in 2008, up from $14.8 billion in 2005, according to R.K. Hammer, a consulting firm. The industry's pretax profit climbed to about $39 billion in 2008 from $30.6 billion in 2005.

(Source: www.usatoday.com/money/economy/2009-03-22-reform-filings-bankruptcy_N.htm)

So the credit card giants are making a profit off the cash-strapped hard working citizen. Same old song and dance.

And did they change their fee policy? Of course not! They drove the knife in harder and gave it a twist. The experts concur:

> "There has been no rollback on credit card fees," says Robert McKinley, founder of CardTrak.com. "Punitive rates are just as aggressive as they were before, even though the prime rate has dropped dramatically. In 2005, the punitive rate was 30.99%

as the prime rate was up to 7.00%. Last year, the punitive credit card rate was 30.88%, but the prime rate was only 4.00%, ... an unprecedented rate spread."

(Source: www.usatoday.com/money/economy/2009-03-22-reform-filings-bankruptcy_N.htm)

Who is benefiting

If you don't believe me, take it straight from the horse's mouth:

"The data is unambiguous: 2005 Bankruptcy Reform benefited credit card companies and hurt their customers."

That was from a report from a Harvard Law School Fellow. He was quoted in the same *USA Today* article that I referenced above.

Same old, same old. The credit card companies get the benefit. The customers get the bill.

Hear it from real people

Once again, the comments that people post to these articles are eye-opening and affirming of everything that I am telling you.

A bankruptcy judge of twenty-five years said, "The 2005 bill was the culmination of 8 years and some $50 million of effort by the finance industry to screw honest debtors. The reference in the title to the legislation as a "Consumer Protection Act" was a fraud and a cruel joke. There are no consumer protections of significance in the Act. There are, however, numerous hurdles and costly measures that serve no purpose other than to shut out distressed individual debtors."

And all of us shake our heads in agreement. You can read the discussion for yourself at www.usatoday.com/money/economy/2009-03-22-reform-filings-bankruptcy_N.htm.

But what if ...?

I tend to say too much and for those of you in the belly of bankruptcy or near bankruptcy, I am not telling you anything that you don't already know. So what if bankruptcy is your option? Let's talk about that.

Bankruptcy is not evil. It is not eternal damnation. It is what it is. And if it is your reality right now, you need to know the hard facts.

> People in their golden years are now facing dire straits and that is just wrong and sad.

Something new and disturbing is the number of bankruptcy filings by folks who are age 55 and older. People in their golden years are now facing dire straits and that is just wrong and sad.

An AARP study found that the increase in filings by this age demographic was up an astonishing 78% over the last ten years. Harvard Law professor Elizabeth Warren was one of the researchers in the study. She states that in 1991, this age group accounted for about 8% of all bankruptcies.

Now? 25%!

Is it you?

I don't know your age, your income, or what phase of life you are in, but I do know that bankruptcy is common. If you are in this group, here is what you need to know.

Get a lawyer. Find someone you trust. Ask around. This situation is more common than you may realize. Your friends, family, and neighbors can probably suggest a good bankruptcy attorney.

The ones who seem shady probably are; trust your gut. You want someone who is looking out for you, not out to make a buck off of you. There are tons that advertise on television and on the internet. Get a recommendation first before you start to deal with him or her and especially before you give any money.

Think about it

Bankruptcy should not be a rash decision. Think about it. Talk about it. Research your options. If you cannot make the house payment and the car payment, that's one factor. If you are not able to pay your bills and pay down on your debt, that's one factor. If you live in fear of answering the phone or opening your mail because you are hounded by collectors, that's one factor.

You need to weigh all the factors.

If you had a serious illness, or lost your job, or had a divorce, or a death, or some other "big" event that created a huge financial mess, you may need to consider bankruptcy. Some people think it is the only option; it is not, but it is an out sometimes.

Some people can't function when they are burdened with debt. If you are one of those people, you need to talk to a lawyer. You need to get your life back.

Fees

There are no set fees so I cannot tell you how much it will cost to file bankruptcy. The costs depend upon your state, and even within states, it is different. Jurisdiction dictates fees and from court to court, judge to judge, you pay differently. What we in California pay is probably different from what you would pay in Colorado or Connecticut.

Some courts place a cap on fees. The internet may or may not give you an accurate estimation. You need to talk to someone in your area.

Maybe you will pay $500. Maybe $1,500. Maybe $3,000. There is no way for me to say.

Simple Simon

I try to keep examples simple because that is what works for me. There are two kinds of individual bankruptcy, Chapter 7 and Chapter 13.

Chapter 7 is a basic liquidation of your assets. What you have is not enough cash value and cannot pay off what you owe, your liabilities. Chapter 13 bankruptcy is called a personal reorganization. With this plan, you pay back your debts over three to five years with a court-approved arrangement.

The type of bankruptcy that you file depends upon your income and your assets and if you want to keep your house. The bankruptcy reform of 2005 wants more people to file Chapter 13 (obviously) instead of letting you wipe the slate clean.

Time

It used to be that if you filed bankruptcy, you had to wait seven years until you could file again. The reform changed the time span to eight years. But with all this kind of legal stuff, check with your attorney.

Filing for bankruptcy does show up as a negative item on the credit report. It stays there for ten years. But if you are in the spot and you feel bankruptcy is the way to go, you can overcome the credit score.

You also have to remember that filing bankruptcy does not knock you down to automatic zero owed. If you have student loans or owe money to the IRS, you still have to pay those debts. Some things just don't go away.

It's your call

Take out a piece of paper and list all your assets. List everything that you owe money on. How does it look?

You can have an accountant draw up an income statement and balance sheet for you, or you can do a rough draft yourself. If the numbers alarm you and make you physically sick, maybe you need to talk to an attorney.

Another word for bankrupt is insolvent. That doesn't sound quite so intimidating, does it? You don't have to throw yourself to the ground, weeping, "I'm ruined. I'm penniless. I'm flat busted, broke."

> Where there is a will to succeed, there is a debt cure to fit the bill.

You decide if being insolvent means talking to a bankruptcy lawyer or if it means pursuing other avenues.

Secret to success

Where there is a will to succeed, there is a debt cure to fit the bill. If bankruptcy is what fits your bill, it is just a blip on your radar and this, too, shall pass.

I am living proof that a person can overcome just about any hard time that comes their way. I know people who live lives now beyond their wildest dreams and they once were in bankruptcy.

It does not mean failure. It does not mean a permanent setback. It means you are insolvent and this is the way to handle it right now.

At the end of the road, you'll see the light. And while you're in the tunnel, you'll find that it's not so dark after all.

Don't forget to try the ways to quick cash—AND now how about looking into some FREE MONEY?! Turn the page.

CHAPTER 22

Free Money

*"I spent 90% of my money on women and drink.
The rest I wasted."*

\- George Best

When I first started writing books, I had no idea that this concept of "free money" would become my passion. And it's not just a concept, it's a reality!

The first *Debt Cures* book launched my quest to find sources of free money for you. I have learned that there are countless grants and loans available from the government and private foundations.

Nothing makes me happier than telling you about free funds from the feds. We here at the Debt Cures team keep finding more places and information. That is why we recently did an entire book, *Kevin Trudeau's Free Money They Don't Want You to Know About*. Call the toll free number or check the website to get your copy! And since information is always changing and more sources are becoming available, subscribe to the monthly newsletter!

For now, let me share what the print space allows.

www.govbenefits.gov

This is a great site to find grants and assistance. There are literally thousands of government programs available and most people have no idea that they even exist. Now you do. Take a click and see what you think.

You do not have to give your confidential, private information, but by filling out a short survey, you can learn what kinds of programs are available to you. Navigating this site is easy and an immense time saver. Trying to research each grant independently would be maddening. To have a one-stop shopping sort of site is very helpful.

You can use the Quick Search feature. Click on a topic; grants and programs in that category are listed. Some of the categories include:

- ✔ Awards;
- ✔ Counseling;
- ✔ Disaster Relief;
- ✔ Financial Assistance;
- ✔ Grants, Scholarships, Fellowships;
- ✔ Housing;
- ✔ Loans;
- ✔ Social Security/Pension;
- ✔ Child Care;
- ✔ Disability Assistance;
- ✔ Education;
- ✔ Food;
- ✔ Health Care;
- ✔ Insurance;
- ✔ Medicare;
- ✔ Utilities

That should give you an indication of the vastness of this site and of our federal government programs. By answering a few brief questions, you can find out if you are eligible for any grants or loans or assistance programs. There is over $400 billion in grant money that gets awarded.

There are hundreds of grant programs from twenty-six different government agencies on this site. It certainly may be worth a few minutes of your time to take a look for yourself.

Navigation

There are two ways to navigate this site. Let's assume you have no idea what you might qualify for or what you are looking for specifically. Most people are like that. Click on the "Start Here" button.

> There is over $400 billion in grant money that gets awarded.

The next screen is an easy-to-answer list of 46 questions. Don't worry, it will take you only five to ten minutes to complete. The questions are simple and straightforward, and completely anonymous. You do not give your name or social security number. The only personal questions are age, gender, and income level.

After you answer the questions, a list of possible grant or benefit programs pops up that you could be eligible for—how simple is that! A friend of mine was questioning whether or not he could qualify for any grants. After all, he's a millionaire. Aren't these grants only for "poor" people? He qualified for seven grants! If he can do it, so can you.

Search feature

The search engine built in to this website is a great tool. Take some time to do your own search and it just might surprise you to find all the programs you can apply to. I do not know how these grants were handled before we had internet technology, but I do know that the web saves hours upon countless hours of time and frustration when it comes to locating possible money sources.

www.grants.gov

Another amazing website for government grants is www.grants. gov. To just browse through all the information, registration is not required. If you want to apply for a grant, you will have to register. (It's free.)

The Small Business Administration (SBA) has many wonderful programs that you can explore. They give out grants as well as loans. The loans often have super terms and incredible interest rates; SBA loans can usually beat any bank in town. Although it is a loan and you will have to repay, it is a sensational deal, and again, worth checking out.

For a quick link, try www.sba.gov/services.

The SBA also has women's business centers. The Small Business Association's Office of Women's Business Ownership focus is to help women achieve their dreams and improve their communities by providing assistance for starting a business.

The SBA provides training on how to get started and how to maintain a successful business, and they provide assistance as you go. Check out the SBA's website for all the details (www.sba.gov/aboutsba/ sbaprograms/onlinewbc/index.html).

For a list of addresses, websites, and email contacts for each state, see: www.sba.gov/idc/groups/public/documents/sba_program_office/ sba_pr_wbc_ed.pdf

SBA's Women Business Centers (WBC) provide resource centers across the nation to help women get their businesses launched and to be available for guidance every step of the way. Grants are available for five years, with the option to renew for another five years. The program's mission is to "level the playing field." These grants are offered to new businesses and existing businesses looking to expand.

www.usa.gov

The official website of the federal government, USA.gov, also contains valuable information about all US government agencies and their various grants.

Click on Benefits and Grants. This link gives you information on grants, loans, financial aid and other benefits. You can even sign up to be notified when the benefit page is updated.

www.govloans.gov

This is another federal government site focusing on loan information, not grants. It is an excellent source for locating loans for children, agriculture, business, disaster relief, education, housing, veterans, or just about anything for which you might need a loan.

www.grantsolutions.gov

Another site to try is www.grantsolutions.gov. This is the web address for the Grants Center of Excellence (COE), a partnership between agencies within Health and Human Services, Department of Agriculture, the Denali Commission, and Department of Treasury.

The COE states that these partner agencies distribute over $250 billion in grants each year. The COE serviced over $58 billion of those grants in fiscal year 2006, which is about 13% of all US grants.

Women

The Women's Financial Fund offers business grants of up to $5,000. They do not look at your credit report so take a deep breath there. Their website explains that the money is a grant and not a loan. Therefore, your ability to pay it back is not an issue.

Getting a grant is a great way to launch your dreams. Visit their website at www.womensbusinessgrants.com/who.shtml.

Another opportunity for women is a loan program of up to $10,000 for women in business (www.count-me-in.org). Also see: www.lib.msu.edu/harris23/grants/3women.htm; www.fundsnetservices.com/women.htm; or www.womensnet.net; plus a host of others. Another helpful resource, www.ehome-basedbusiness.com/articles, provides a list of 25 important telephone numbers for those launching a business.

Foundations

> ...there are foundations with money to give away. That is the whole purpose of their existence.

Besides government grants, there are foundations with money to give away. That is the whole purpose of their existence. If they exist just to give funds, don't you want to be on the list of possible contenders?

Do your research and see if you qualify. There are thousands of grants and each has its own set of requirements. Doing a little window shopping on the foundations is very interesting. You may come across something that fits you or maybe you'll find something for someone you know. Be sure to pass on the good news.

Some sites worth your time:
- ✔ www.foundationcenter.org/getstarted/individuals/
- ✔ www.fundsnetservices.com
- ✔ www.kn.pacbell.com/products/grants/locate.html
- ✔ www.foundations.org

I am a big believer in foundations, and these private sources can often be a terrific source of funds. The sites listed above are just an example of what is out there. Suffice to say, it is overwhelming.

Private foundations, government (all levels: federal, state, county, and local) and corporations all have grant money and assistance loans that they want to give away. They want to give it away! All you need to do is apply. (For the ones that you are eligible for, of course. If the grant is for a salmon fisherman in Alaska and you are not a salmon fisherman in Alaska, you won't get the grant so don't waste anyone's time. Go find the grants for a photographer in Virginia, or female business owner, or rural homeowner, or whatever, and apply for what you qualify for.)

You have nothing to lose. Ask and you just may receive.

Students

There are many grant opportunities for those pursuing higher education. Some grants are for traditional college age students, and others are not. If getting your education has been your dream, go find a grant!

If you think that you can't afford college, think again. There is probably a program for you. Check out these sites:

- ✔ www.studentaid.ed.gov
- ✔ www.ed.gov/programs/iegpsirs/index.html
- ✔ www.ed.gov/about/offices/list/fsa/index.html
- ✔ www.ed.gov/about/offices/list/ope/iegps/index.html

Many students long to study abroad. There are many grants, scholarships, and fellowships available.

Boren Scholarships provide up to $20,000 for an academic year's study abroad. Boren Fellowships provide up to $30,000 for language study and international research.

See ourworld.worldlearning.org/site/News2?id=9133&page=
NewsArticle.

There are many, many more including:
- ✔ www.StudyAbroadFunding.org
- ✔ FederalFundingPrograms.org
- ✔ IIEPassport.org

Paying the Bills

You also need to be aware that there are grant and loan programs to help with paying utility bills, child care, and grocery bills. There are organizations that give such "emergency" money. It can help you to bridge the gap to use this assistance, and to help keep your monthly expenditures under control.

Don't forget about these options and don't be too proud to take advantage of all that is available. The programs exist. Use them!

If you are disabled or if you are a senior citizen, Social Security has a branch that can help you. Funded by the general tax coffers, Supplemental Security Income (SSI) exists to aid seniors, the blind, and the disabled in paying off their everyday expenses.

Blind and disabled children can apply as well. It is an income-based program. The less income you have, the more aid you can qualify for. If you are eligible, fill out an application. You can use these dollars to pay off your bills.

The SSI sends out checks *every month* to help people pay off their expenses. You can receive up to thousands of dollars a year. Now isn't that worth knowing? Even if you don't qualify, maybe you know someone who does. Share what you know.

Call Social Security at 1-800-772-1213 to see if you meet the current income requirements. You can also learn more and apply at: www.socialsecurity.gov/ssi/text-understanding-ssi.htm.

The monthly benefit rates change each year. Some states will even add to the federal benefits that SSI is already giving. It is nice when two sources work in cooperation. So pay attention. If you qualify for SSI, you may also qualify for certain additional services within your state.

State governments have many programs that exist to give you a helping hand. For example, Arizona Public Service (APS) has a program that helps low-income residents pay their energy bills.

> The savings on your energy costs can give you money to use to pay off loans or credit cards.

Qualified individuals can get a discount of up to 40% off. They look at your household income and how much energy you use to calculate what you pay. The savings on your energy costs can give you money to use to pay off loans or credit cards.

For more information, visit www.aps.com. You can also call 1-800-582-5706 to find out more about eligibility requirements.

Whatever state you live in, research the programs that are available to you. There are also federally funded energy assistance programs. The Low Income Home Energy Assistance Program (LIHEAP), run by the Division of Energy Assistance, is a great place to go if you're looking for some funds to pay your energy bills. Their program's dollars are distributed among all fifty states. Check to see if you can qualify within your state. Get more information here: www.acf.hhs.gov/programs/liheap.

Besides energy bills, you have other utilities that need to be paid. Your state may offer an assistance program. Pick up the phone and ask. I know you have learned by now that great and surprising things come to those who ask. Call the utility office in your state. You never know—you may be able to receive significant discounts on all your utilities.

Child care

There are a number of programs available to help you with child care expenses. Anyone with children knows how expensive day care can be. When the kids start school and the parent no longer has to pay the large day care bill every month, there is a large boost to the monthly income. Think if you could get some assistance now to boost your income.

The Office of Family Assistance (OFA) operates the Temporary Assistance for Needy Families (TANF) program. This program has been in existence since 1997. It provides free job training and education, and helps with locating grants that pay for child care.

By contacting state agencies, the OFA can find a program that is right for you. You can learn more at: www.acf.hhs.gov/programs/ofa/. Also, be sure to check out some other opportunities at: www.childcareaware.org or www.workfamily.org.

Working parents have so much to juggle and the stress level can get so high. Find out all your options and pursue them. If there is cash available, don't you want it to be yours?

The U.S. Department of Health and Human Services is responsible for another organization that may be able to help you. The Child Care and Development Block Grant (CCDBG) provides funds to assist with child care costs as well.

Every year, families can receive up to thousands of dollars to pay their day care costs. Parents are allowed to choose their own child care provider, as long as it is a legal operation and it meets all state health and safety requirements.

More information can be found at: www.naeyc.org/policy/federal/ccdbg.asp or www.nccic.org.

Take action

The recurring theme throughout all my books, seminars, and teaching is that you must act. I can tell you information and you can take notes and get excited. You need enthusiasm, but having the knowledge gets you nowhere if you do not put it to use.

Learning that grants are available is good. Applying for grants is even better. Fill out the applications and send them off. Many are able to be done via the internet. It's quick and it's free and it's immediate.

When you are writing your grant application, be yourself and be passionate. Don't try to sound like anything different than who you are. In an earlier chapter, I talked about envisioning your brightest future and following your heart. Those concepts apply here as well.

Grants usually have to be straight to the point and not very wordy. There are people who specialize in writing grants. If you need help, contact the agency directly or hire a grant writer, if the amount is enough to warrant paying for that service. Most of the time you can follow the directions and do it all yourself.

Apply

A million people every year get money from the government, either through grants or loans. Did you have any idea there was that much money available and that there were that many different programs? There is something out there for you.

Read about grants and low cost loans. Ask people. Surf the internet. A little information can take you a very long way.

There are hundreds and thousands of programs offered every year. Some have specific restrictions as to how you must spend the money; some do not. Getting the money could even be easier than you would expect. Phone calls and filling out applications are usually all it takes.

Some grants require lots of paperwork, but you can find grants that merely require an easy-to-complete form with information you already know. Whatever office is giving the grant can answer any of your questions. They are happy to work with you.

There are many specific, more narrow grants as well, and there are places that exist simply to offer a helping hand. Perhaps you find yourself in a position where you are now looking for work and you do not have appropriate clothes. Most every state has a program like www.dressforsuccess.org and www.bottomlesscloset.org that can provide you with interview outfits and the clothes are yours to keep.

Organizations like that are tremendous. They discovered a need and filled it. And also what I find fulfilling is how a local community program can become a national force. There is power in good deeds.

Class action

Another little known source of free money is the class action lawsuit. You may be party to some money and not be aware of it. For example, maybe your utility company mischarged for years. A class action lawsuit can be brought against the company. That means not one person is suing, but the suit is filed on behalf of everyone it affects. Everyone who paid their bills during that timeframe of the overcharges is entitled to a refund of these charges in the class action suit.

There are suits being filed all the time and you may be included. When you get a letter in the mail that says you are part of a class action suit, do not toss it in the trash. There usually is a short form to fill out and return. Do it. What have you got to lose?

The settlement portion that comes your way could be a few bucks, or it could be big bucks! And instead of waiting for a letter to appear in your mailbox, you can actively search class action suits that might pertain to you. Visit www.topclassactions.com.

Money can come from anywhere, at any time! Be on the lookout!

CHAPTER 23

More Money From Uncle Sam (and Others)

Uncle Sam wants you! Wants to give you money!

I am no fan of the Internal Revenue Service, no secret there. But there is money available to you from the IRS, Uncle Sam, and others, and it is my job to share that information with you. There are tax credits that are, essentially, a gift from the government. Money is money, and money from the feds is always a delight.

Lost money

Or should I say FOUND MONEY?! There are thousands upon thousands of dollars that literally could have your name on it. You are entitled to what is yours! Maybe it is old savings bonds that you forgot about, or an old bank account. There are many sources of "forgotten" money and that money is just sitting waiting to be claimed.

There was $12.5 billion in value of unclaimed savings bonds as of 2005. As of March 2009, the US Savings Bond Search page says that the amount is now over $15 billion. $15 billion!

That $15 billion is comprised of about 35 million bonds. Are you the holder of any those 35 million? Go to unclaimedasssets.com and find out! (Try missingmoney.com too!)

Goldmine

This website—unclaimedassets.com—is a veritable goldmine. There are many places holding unclaimed assets and some of those assets may find their way back to you. (I am so excited about this goldmine and all the FREE MONEY sources I found that I wrote a book about it. *Kevin Trudeau's Free Money They Don't Want You to Know About!* This is just a tiny sampling of what I share in that book.)

Besides lost United States savings bonds, there are bank accounts, pension accounts, social security checks, veterans benefits, life insurance, and the list goes on and on. There are store refunds and rebates waiting to be claimed. There are BILLIONS of dollars and MILLIONS of people who need to find each other!

Most of these web links require just a name and social security number to do the check for you. It's so quick and so easy. I even found money coming to me that I didn't know about! I have a very wealthy friend who found lost money in his name, too! Income doesn't matter—if it is yours, it's yours! Claim it!

Tax refunds

A great free money source is old tax refunds that you have waiting for you. Uncle Sam didn't find you, but you may be due some dough from years past. There is over A BILLION bucks in unclaimed tax refunds. Maybe some of that is yours!

You simply go online to www.irs.gov and click on "Where's my refund." To research the missing refund, you need to know your social security number, your filing status (married filing joint, single, married filing separate, head of household, or qualifying widow/er), and the dollar amount of the refund you are expecting. (FYI – Always keep a copy of your tax returns!)

The IRS folks will look into your situation and see what happened to your money. Many times it is because they cannot deliver your check. The IRS does not allow mail to be forwarded. If this is the problem with your account, you can go online to update your current address.

If you have an IRS taxpayer service office in your town, you can always mosey in with proof of ID and ask them to look up your past years and make sure there is no unpaid money sitting in their coffers that should be in your pockets.

Tax credits

First Time Homebuyers Tax Credit

This credit is new and is a result of our tumultuous economy. Because it is new, many people are not aware of it or how it works. It is confusing because if you buy a house in 2009, you can claim this credit on your 2008 tax return or your 2009 return.

If you are a first time homebuyer, 2009 looks to be a good year. Home prices are historically low and foreclosure bargains are everywhere. This new $8,000 credit applies to a home purchased in 2009 (before December 1, 2009), so if you are thinking about buying, it could be an added incentive.

> This new $8,000 credit applies to a home purchased in 2009 (before December 1, 2009)

Eight grand is not chump change. Even if you have already filed your 2008 return, there are ways to still claim this credit this year. I say get your money back as soon as possible. If you are a first time homebuyer, and there should be a lot of you this year, listen up.

From the Treasury website: "Under the American Recovery and Reinvestment Act of 2009, qualifying taxpayers who purchase a home before December 1 receive up to $8,000, or $4,000 for married individuals filing separately. People can claim the credit either on their 2008 tax returns due April 15 or on their 2009 tax returns next year." [Source: www.irs.gov/newsroom/article/0,,id=205416,00.html]

The credit is up to $8,000 ($4,000 if you are married filing separately). You are allowed to deduct ten percent of the purchase price of the home up to that $8,000 limit. If you find a home for $50,000, you can claim a credit of $5,000. If you find a home for $90,000, you are limited to the max credit of $8,000—not the 10% which would be $9,000. But hey, eight grand is pretty grand! Maybe I should remind you that a tax credit is not a deduction. It completely wipes out tax. If you owed $8,000 in taxes but were eligible for the max $8,000 credit, you would owe ZERO—a big fat 0—in tax.

This one is a little confusing because you can take it in 2008 even though the home purchase happens in 2009. The filing options per www.irs.gov are:

- ✔ **File an extension.** Taxpayers who haven't yet filed their 2008 returns, but are buying a home soon, can request a six-month extension to October 15. This step would be faster than waiting until next year to claim it on the 2009 tax return. Even with an extension, taxpayers could still file electronically, receiving their refund in as few as 10 days with direct deposit.

- ✔ **File now, amend later.** Taxpayers due a sizable refund for their 2008 tax return, but who also are considering buying a house in the next few months, can file their return now and claim the credit later. Taxpayers would file their 2008 tax forms as usual, then follow up with an amended return later this year to claim the homebuyer credit.

- ✔ **Amend the 2008 tax return.** Taxpayers buying a home in the near future who have already filed their 2008 tax return

can consider filing an amended tax return. The amended tax
return will allow them to claim the homebuyer credit on the
2008 return without waiting until next year to claim it on the
2009 return.

✔ **Claim the credit in 2009 rather than 2008.** For some
taxpayers, it may make more financial sense to wait and claim
the homebuyer credit next year when they file the 2009 tax
return rather than claiming it now on the 2008 tax return. This
could benefit taxpayers who might qualify for a higher credit
on the 2009 tax return. This could include people who have
less income in 2009 than 2008 because of factors such as a job
loss or drop in investment income.

[Source: www.irs.gov/newsroom/article/0,,id=205416,00.html]

Be advised that you get less credit as your income goes up. If you
are married filing jointly and make more than $150,000, you will not
be able to take the full credit. If you are single and make more than
$75,000, you will not be able to take the max credit either. Well, I
am simplifying a bit when I say "if you make more than $xx." That
figure is adjusted gross income, which is not the exact amount of your
wages. If you are over the income limits and need help determining
the maximum credit you are allowed, see the website, give the IRS a
call, or ask your tax man.

This credit comes to us because of the American Recovery and
Reinvestment Act, part of the new Obama administration. Visit www.
Recovery.gov to learn more. This is what they—the people who wrote
the act—have to say about it:

The American Recovery and Reinvestment Act is an unprecedented effort to jumpstart our economy, create or save millions
of jobs, and put a down payment on addressing long-neglected
challenges so our country can thrive in the 21st century. The
Recovery and Reinvestment Act is an extraordinary response
to a crisis unlike any since the Great Depression. With much

at stake, the Act provides for unprecedented levels of transparency and accountability so that you will be able to know how, when, and where your tax dollars are being spent. Spearheaded by a new Recovery Board, this Act contains built-in measures to root out waste, inefficiency, and unnecessary spending. This website, Recovery.gov, will be the main vehicle to provide each and every citizen with the ability to monitor the progress of the recovery. [Source: www.Recovery.gov]

Lofty and wordy, yes, but an eight grand tax credit is a beautiful thing.

Child Tax Credit

I get a kick out of "IRS language." How does this sentence work for you: "You may be able to claim the child tax credit if you have a qualifying child"?

Hmm. You got kids? Let's see if they qualify as a "qualifying child."

1. Is a United States citizen or resident, or national;

2. Is under age 17 at the end of the calendar year;

3. Is your son, daughter, stepson, stepdaughter, legally adopted child, or a child placed with you for legal adoption, brother, sister, stepbrother, stepsister, foster child, or a descendant of any such person; AND

4. Shares with you the same principal residence for more than one-half of the tax year, or is treated as your qualifying child under the special rule for parents who are divorced, separated, or living apart.

You know what's funny? I tried to make those four qualifiers simpler to understand and they still sound a bit over the top. In # 4, I used the word "residence." The IRS used "place of abode."

Basically, for most of you, assuming you are a US citizen, if your child is still under age 17, you probably meet the requirements for "qualifying child." If you claim that kid as yours at the family picnic, you probably meet the requirements.

If your fifteen-year-old comes home pierced and tattooed and dyed her hair black and white, you may gasp, "That's not my kid." For purposes of the child tax credit, however, you will want to claim her.

What is the child tax credit? A little bonus in your pocket for those expensive offspring. Kids cost big bucks to clothe and feed. A little tax credit back your way is a good thing. If you want some in-depth reading on this credit, pick up Publication 672. If you have questions, as always, call the IRS or look up www.irs.gov.

> A little tax credit back your way is a good thing.

In a nutshell, you get a credit of $1,000 per little darling. If you have one child, your credit is $1,000 (limited to income restrictions that will phase out the credit the more money you make. Married filing jointly, the income limit is $110,000; and single, it is $75,000).

If your tax due is $1,000, you apply the credit and dollar for dollar wipe out the tax. You owe nothing. If your tax bill was $1,400, you would only owe $400.

This credit is not refundable. That means if you owe $500 in tax and your credit is $1,000, you eliminate all tax, but do not get the extra $500 refunded to you.

Some credits are refundable. Even if you owe no tax, you still get the full credit money. Now that I really like!

To claim the credit, it is as easy as checking a box on the front of the return where you enter the names and social security numbers of your children.

Earned Income Tax Credit

The Earned Income Tax Credit (EITC) is a refundable credit. That means if you qualify for this credit, file your tax return! You get the money! This is one of the reasons the Treasury is bulging with unclaimed money. EITC folks are not filing to get their fair share.

The key words here are earned income. That means a job. If you have income that you earned from working, check into the requirements for this credit. And in case you were wondering, you do not have to have a child to qualify for this credit. You just have to have earned income.

The basic rules for this credit are:

✔ Must have a valid Social Security Number.

✔ You must have earned income from employment or from self-employment.

✔ Your filing status cannot be married filing separately.

✔ You must be a U.S. citizen or resident alien all year, or a nonresident alien married to a U.S. citizen or resident alien and filing a joint return.

✔ You **cannot** be a qualifying child of another person.

✔ If you do not have a qualifying child, you must:

    o be age 25 but under 65 at the end of the year,

    o live in the United States for more than half the year, and

    o not qualify as a dependent of another person.

Okay. I think I've got that figured out. The next hurdle is income requirements.

For tax year 2008:

Earned income and adjusted gross income (AGI) must each be less than:

✔ $38,646 ($41,646 married filing jointly) with two or more qualifying children;

✔ $33,995 ($36,995 married filing jointly) with one qualifying child;

✔ $12,880 ($15,880 married filing jointly) with no qualifying children.

Tax year 2008 maximum credit:

✔ $4,824 with two or more qualifying children;

✔ $2,917 with one qualifying child;

✔ $438 with no qualifying children.

And last but not least, investment income must be $2,950 or less.

Go to www.irs.gov to check the dollar amounts for each year, or if you have questions. Credits can be tricky to understand. Sometimes the IRS gets a little long-winded in their explanations and I have succumbed to that, too.

Remember, if you have questions, call the toll-free IRS number or ask a friend or take advantage of the free local tax help. These credits are great money for you! Be sure to take advantage, if they apply to you!

You can see that you do not have to have a child for this credit but if you do, you get more credit. Give that kid a hug. If you are married and file together and have two kids, you can get over $4,800 in free money. Holy cow! That could be a huge help to the household!

For tax year 2009 (due April 15, 2010), the money amounts are:

✔ $40,295 ($43,415 married filing jointly) with two or more qualifying children;

✔ $35,463 ($38,583 married filing jointly) with one qualifying child;

✔ $13,440 ($16,560 married filing jointly) with no qualifying children.

Tax year 2009 maximum credit:

✔ $5,028 with two or more qualifying children;

✔ $3,043 with one qualifying child;

✔ $457 with no qualifying children.

I cannot stress enough how many people are entitled to this EITC and do not claim it. If you want to read more, get IRS Publication 596. If you qualify for EITC, you may also be entitled to a similar credit on your state tax return.

> If you qualify for EITC, you may also be entitled to a similar credit on your state tax return.

For the list of states that offer EITC (there are twenty-two as we go to print), check out www.irs.gov/individuals/article/0,,id=177866,00.html.

Before I move on to the next credit, there is one more thing you need to know about EITC. You can get a little advance credit in your paycheck throughout the year instead of waiting for the tax return. Yep! It is called Advance Earned Income Tax Credit.

There is a form you fill out and give to your employer if you expect to qualify and have at least one child. A little extra in the paycheck is a nice option if you want to take advantage of it. When you file your tax return at the end of the year, report the amount of the credit you have already received (it will be on your W-2 earnings statement from your employer) and file for the rest of the credit due you.

Visit www.irs.gov/individuals/article/0,,id=96466,00.html for all the detailed info on the Earned Income Tax Credit.

Credit for Child and Dependent Care Expenses

Do you pay someone to care for your kids who are under age 13 so you can go to work? Do you pay someone to care for your spouse or your dependent who cannot care for himself/herself? You may be entitled to a credit of 20% to 35% of those expenses.

For all the details, see Publication 503 or www.irs.gov. The same kind of rules for "qualifying" children apply.

In general, if you work and pay day care, this credit is for you. You will have to identify the caregiver on the form and give the social security number if you pay an individual or tax ID number if you use a day care center.

Paying a babysitter while you go to Bunco night does not count here. Paying a babysitter while you work, or look for work, does count here. Follow the instructions for Form 2441 and it walks you through to easily compute the credit.

The credit varies from person to person because it is based on what you pay for child care and what your earned income is. For example, if you pay $3,000 for Little Junior's day care and your income is over $43,000, you get 20% of the $3,000 as your credit, $600. And that is nothing to sneeze at.

If you pay $6,000 for two kids to go to day care while you work and have income less than $15,000, your credit is 35% of the $6,000. My math computes that to be a credit of $2,100. Nice found money!

The form shows the income limits and the percentage you are allowed. The total credit is limited to $5,000.

Education Tax Credits

Education tax credits can help offset the costs of higher education for you or your dependent. Schooling is not cheap and you need every break that comes your way. If you or your student is enrolled at least half time, check out these credits.

The Hope Credit applies for the first two years of college or vocational school. The credit can be up to $1,800 per student per year. If you have gone back to school and have a kid in college, you get double dips.

The second credit available is called the Lifetime Learning Credit. This credit applies to undergrad, graduate, and professional level degrees. It is not just the first two years like the Hope Credit.

This credit is 20% of the first $10,000 you pay in tuition and fees, up to a maximum of $2,000 per year.

You cannot claim the Hope Credit and the Lifetime Learning Credit for the same student in the same year. But if you have more than one student in your household, it is possible to claim both credits.

Watch the income limits. If you are married filing jointly and your income is over $116,000, you do not get these education credits. If your income is between $96,000 and $116,000, the amount of the credit is reduced.

To get the full scoop, check out www.irs.gov or get Publication 970. The form to claim these credits is Form 8863.

In case I have not mentioned it, all forms and publications are available for download at www.irs.gov.

Saver's Credit

The purpose of this credit is to help workers save for retirement and get a tax break now. If you put money into an IRA (Individual Retirement Account) or your employer's 401(k) plan, this Saver's Credit may apply to you.

The credit can be claimed by:

✔ Married couples filing jointly with incomes up to $53,000 in 2008 or $55,500 in 2009;

✔ Heads of Household with incomes up to $39,750 in 2008 or $41,625 in 2009; and

✔ Married individuals filing separately and singles with incomes up to $26,500 in 2008 or $27,750 in 2009.

Like other tax credits, the saver's credit can increase a taxpayer's refund or reduce the tax owed. Gotta love those tax credits. The maximum Saver's Credit is $1,000 for single filers and $2,000 for married couples.

A taxpayer's credit amount is based on filing status, adjusted gross income, tax liability, and amount contributed to qualifying retirement programs. Form 8880 is used to claim the saver's credit, and the instructions have details on how to figure the credit.

Per the IRS: For tax year 2006, the most recent year for which figures are available, saver's credits totaling almost $900 million were claimed on nearly 5.2 million individual income tax returns. Saver's credits claimed on these returns averaged $213 for joint filers, $149 for heads of household, and $128 for single filers.

What else you need to know to claim this credit:

✔ Eligible taxpayers must be at least 18 years of age.

✔ Anyone claimed as a dependent on someone else's return cannot take the credit.

✔ A student cannot take the credit. A person enrolled as a full-time student during any part of 5 calendar months during the year is considered a student.

Begun in 2002 as a temporary provision, the saver's credit was made a permanent part of the tax code in legislation enacted in 2006. To help preserve the value of the credit, income limits are now adjusted annually to keep pace with inflation. More information about the credit is on www.irs.gov (www.irs.gov/newsroom/article/0,,id=200742,00.html).

Maybe I have rattled on a bit long about tax credits, but think about it! With all the ways that the government puts the screws to us, tax credits are one way we can collect what is our due! If you qualify for a tax credit, file your return and claim it! Unclaimed money goes back to the US Treasury. Shouldn't it go in your pocket instead?

Before I get off the topic of taxes, there is one more found money bonanza I need to tell you about. Did you know that you can deduct the sales tax you paid on the purchase of a new car?

Sales Tax Deduction for Vehicle Purchases

This is another new "recovery tool" that came to pass this year. The American Recovery and Reinvestment Act of 2009 allows you to take a deduction for the sales tax and any excise tax you paid on a new car, light truck, motorcycle, or motor home through 2009. Depending on the state and the purchase price, that can be a pretty hefty amount.

Even if you don't use Schedule A to itemize your deductions on your tax return, you still get to take this new deduction. Very nice.

There are limits of course. The deduction is limited to tax on $49,500 of the purchase price. If you bought a motor home that costs $50,000, you would have to prorate the tax. If your income is more than $125,000 (single) or $250,000 (married), the deduction is phased out. It gets wiped out completely for incomes exceeding $135,000 or $260,000.

If you made your new car purchase before February 17, 2009, you're screwed and don't get to take this credit. I don't know why they have to do it like that. Just make the deduction apply to the whole calendar year and keep it simple is my thought. But they didn't ask me.

Anyway, tell your friends, neighbors, and anyone you know who made a vehicle purchase to be sure to grab this special deduction.

And don't forget those tax credits!

Other ways to money are all around. Once I get started, I get hooked on exploring the options. You need to be an explorer, too.

Employee plans

Don't overlook your employer when you are mulling over day care costs. Some employers provide day care onsite, but many do not. However, there are a large number of employers out there that offer a plan where you can pay your child care expenses with pre-tax money.

> ...a plan where you can pay your child care expenses with pre-tax money.

The employer takes money out of your paycheck each week that goes toward your day care provider expenses. You do not have to pay tax on this portion of your income. That means big savings at the end of the year.

Contact your employer to find out if this benefit is available to you. Remember, you never know until you ask. Besides child care, many employers offer this same kind of plan for your health and medical expenses. You predict how much you pay during the year for insurance and doctor bills and prescriptions. The employer withholds that from your paycheck and puts it into a spending account.

Tax savings plans

Again, you do not pay income taxes on this portion of your wages, a big dollar advantage, and you have a savings account to pay the doctor bills when they come up. If your company has these types of plans, take advantage of them. Some companies call them cafeteria plans; some call them flexible spending accounts. Talk to the human resource person at your place of employment to see what is offered and all of the terms and conditions.

Aside from child care expenses, raising kids costs a lot of money. Now, that's an understatement!

Preschool

Raising a child brings about all kinds of concerns and considerations. Education is fundamental. There is a program called Head Start that provides free preschool for families who qualify. Head Start provides lower income families with the tools to help the development of their children. The program offers a variety of educational, social, and health services.

These kids get help when they are young and like little sponges, they soak it all up. They can then head off to kindergarten and elementary school with the skills to keep up with all the others kids. The program likes to think of itself as giving children a "head start" on the path toward success. There are also programs now called Even Start that provide the same goals. Go to the web for more information: www2.acf.dhhs.gov/programs/hsb.

Transportation

I also learned of a program run by the Federal Transit Administration that can be a godsend if you're having trouble transporting your child. The program was first organized to provide free transportation to senior citizens and people with disabilities. Within the FTA's "guidance document" (C9070), there is language that plainly states that free transportation can be used by others if they can demonstrate that an unplanned event has left them in a bind.

Let's say your child is suddenly left with no way to get to school and you have no other options. You can try to take advantage of the free transportation available. The FTA hands out millions of dollars a year to local groups in order to fund this free service. That's a lot of money, and if you need the assistance, you shouldn't hesitate in pursuing it. Learn more at www.fta.dot.gov or by calling 202-366-4020.

Adoption

Adoption is a wonderful blessing, but it can be very expensive. If you plan on adoption, you need to know that there are benefits available.

The National Adoption Foundation gives financial assistance. They provide grants, not only to be used toward adopting a child, but toward raising a child as well! Learn more at: www.nafadopt.org.

Back to the IRS and tax credits, did you know about the Adoption Tax Credit? You can get over $10,000 in tax breaks! That's worth knowing about! There are several adoption expenses that qualify for this credit. Get more information here: www.irs.gov/taxtopics/tc607.html.

Adoption is becoming more common with each passing year. Some employers and companies today offer adoption benefits to their employees to help ease the burden of the large costs associated with adoption.

Employer benefits

Check with your employer to find out what your company is offering. If you are planning to adopt, and your company does not have an adoption benefits program, talk to them about implementing one. As I have said over and over again, all you have to do is ask.

Time and time again, I am stunned at what can happen when all you have to do is ask. It only takes one person speaking up to get the ball rolling. You can be that person.

Emergencies—Crisis funds

> There are agencies and organizations that provide assistance when crisis hits.

When we least expect it, something happens from out of the blue and catches us totally off guard. Many Americans do not have any savings at all. When people live paycheck to paycheck and tragedy strikes, there is no back-up plan, no emergency fund.

There are agencies and organizations that provide assistance when crisis hits. If you need money to get by or to pay the bills, pay the rent or pay to get the car fixed, whatever you may need, there are places that can offer you help.

The U.S. Department of Health and Human Services (DHHS) is a good place to start. Operating in ten regions across the country, the DHHS has the goal of maintaining the "health and well-being" of our nation.

DHHS offices vary from region to region, so be sure to check what is available where you live. In the Seattle region, for example, DHHS offers three different kinds of emergency grants. They work with other agencies and organizations to provide housing, medical aid, food, and clothing.

For more information, see: www.wroc.org/factsheets/emergencygrant.htm. To find your region, visit www.dhhs.gov.

Providers in action

The Community Action Partnership is another emergency needs provider. This partnership oversees a network of Community Action Agencies all over the country. These agencies are nonprofit organizations that provide support and financial assistance to low-income families.

They offer community outreach, job training, counseling, food pantries, and transportation programs. To learn more about this network, check them out at: www.communityactionpartnership.com.

And once again, you can go to www.govbenefits.gov to learn more about a whole host of emergency grants. If an emergency strikes and you need help, you can also call local agencies where you can get the number right out of your phone book.

Local agencies

For food and shelter needs, contact the local Salvation Army or your local Red Cross chapter. To learn more, you can go to: www.salvationarmy.org.

Don't forget that your local Public Assistance office may be able to provide the funds that you need. If you need aid, apply for it. In some states, Pubic Aid will offer assistance while you are waiting to receive funds from other grant programs. The amount that is provided differs in each state. Check with your local office when an emergency hits and you need help.

When an emergency befalls you, take advantage of these resources to help get you back on your feet again. And even if you are not in a state of emergency, but need help, there are many more programs available. It is mind-boggling all the money and aid that is out there. It is there. If you can apply, do so.

More help

I am just scratching the surface with all I am sharing here. When you do your own research, you can find programs and organizations that offer assistance for what you are looking for.

It is so intriguing to me that all these opportunities for help even exist. Spending a little of your time surfing the web and reading and asking people questions can reap large rewards for you.

Many times, we think the self-employed person is the only one who can take tax breaks or get some kind of benefits. As you can see, that is not the case. There are benefits for all kinds of employees, too.

Transportation benefits for employees

Have you ever heard that transportation benefits exist? As an employee, you can receive transportation fringe benefits. Taking advantage of these benefits can lead to big savings in your monthly cash flow. When you save money, remember to control it. That means you save it, and do not spend it as "extra" dough.

If you are eligible, you may receive over $100 for transportation costs, or over $200 for parking costs. It does not seem like it could be real, but it is. Tax free funds to help with your day-to-day living expenses!

For more information on this Qualification Transportation Fringe Benefit, go to: www.irs.gov/publications/p15b/ar02.html#d0e2081. Check it out and then talk to your employer to find out how you can start receiving these benefits.

Insurance

I keep hearing that people are giving up their health insurance because it is too expensive. That can be dangerous. I understand the hardship though. Times are tough and you think something has to give somewhere. So you take a gamble and decide that insurance is something you do without.

It's risky business. I hate to think of all the families left unprotected in the face of some unforeseen emergency. Medical bills are even more expensive than insurance.

For folks over the age of 65 who struggle to pay for Medicare coverage, I've got news for you about QMB. QMB is Qualified Medicare Beneficiary, a program aimed toward easing the burden of Medicare payments. The best news is that it's simple to apply for. If you qualify, the benefits are large. They provide payments toward Medicare Part A and Medicare Part B. With co-insurance and deductibles, that is a tremendous reduction in your burden.

Call Medicare at 1-800-MEDICARE (1-800-633-4227), or visit their site at: www.medicare.gov.

Home repair

The programs go on and on. I have learned of a program that gives assistance if you need to repair or modernize your home or if you need to remove safety and health hazards from your house.

That is good news for many people. The Rural Housing Repair Loans and Grants program offers low cost loans of up to $20,000. When I say low cost, I am not exaggerating. The terms can be up to 20 years at 1%.

This program also offers grants—money that you never repay—up to $7,500. And they let you take both so you can get a total of $27,500. If times are tough or your credit is lousy, there are still options out there for you.

This assistance deal is part of a US Department of Agriculture program and applies to rural homeowners. How they define rural may just include you. See www.govbenefits.gov and www.rurdev.usda.gov/rhs/ to get all the information and the application process details.

Family assistance

There are countless programs out there that offer help. Check with your local Family Assistance Administration office (FAA). For example, in Arizona, the FAA administers the Arizona Cash Assistance Program.

This program gives cash for services to kids, families and individuals. Yes, cash. What they do, actually, is give debit cards that work just like cash. Use at ATMs and in most stores. The cash is not debited out of your account, but the cash assistance account.

That is true convenience. Having the cash to spend where and when you need it is an amazing help. Check out www.govbenefits.gov (type in the name of the program, Family Assistance Administration, or your state name followed by cash assistance program, in the search box) to see if you are eligible and to get more information on program requirements and contact information.

To download an application for the Arizona assistance program, visit www.de.state.az.us/faa/appcenter.asp. For questions about this program, call FAA Customer Services at 800-325-8401.

If you want to locate the FAA office closest to your home or where you work, go to www.de.state.az.us/faa/contact.asp. It doesn't cost to search for these programs. There is no application fee. It is worth every effort you make to find cash that you do not have to pay back.

Out of work

Unemployment rates are sky-high all over the nation. People everywhere are losing their jobs. It can be scary and frustrating. To walk into work one morning and that afternoon be told that you are let go can be devastating.

Thousands of people get that news now every day. The first thing you need to do is contact your state unemployment office and file for unemployment.

Every state offers unemployment insurance and you need to take advantage. The days will be filled with job hunting and applications and resumes. You need to make sure that you get some income in the down time.

> If you find yourself in the unemployment ranks, do not despair.

Apply right away

Apply with your state local office. You may be pleasantly surprised when you get that first check. In California, you can receive up to $450 a week. In New York, you can collect up to $405 per week. This is income that you get every week and do not have to repay.

Look at it like a grant from a program that wants to kick-start your life. The amount you get is based on past wages and your particular state's rules. Each state has a cap. In most states, you are allowed to collect unemployment for 26 weeks.

That is just over six months—half a year! That gives you plenty of time to figure out what you want to do next, how to launch your next plan. If you find yourself in the unemployment ranks, do not despair. There is always hope and a better career. This is the time to be envisioning your brightest future.

For more information, visit workforcesecurity.doleta.gov/unemploy/uifactsheet.asp.

See the world

There are grants available for "fun money" as well. No crisis. No loss of job. No emergency need for funds to get the heat turned back on. Sometimes you just want to see the world. To see it on someone else's dime is a dream come true.

The U.S. Department of Education has many programs for students to travel abroad. Foreign language studies and study of other cultures is very important in our global economy. The government wants students and educational institutions to become more involved in the world at large and they provide the funds for travel. That is exciting!

Department of Education

Students and teachers should contact the Department of Education. They provide travel expenses and living expenses while abroad to qualified candidates. You can learn more at: www.ed.gov/ programs/iegpsflasf/index.html.

There are scholarships and fellowships that provide funds for international study. Some awards are up to $20,000 and even $30,000 for study in both the United States and in other countries.

Because the world is smaller now, as they say, and national security is an issue that we didn't talk about before 2001, there are now opportunities that pay if you want to travel to a country that the government feels is important to learn about.

The National Security Education Programs provides fellowships for graduate level students to study languages and cultures that are deemed important to US national security. Students who desire a career in the federal government and wish to take coursework abroad should consider this opportunity.

Fellowships are up to $30,000. Applications are done completely online. See www.borenawards.org/boren_fellowship.

... never ends ...

Obviously, you can see how many programs are available and how the internet is your ticket to assistance. There is so much that I did not mention. It's fun sharing with you all the good news that exists. I just can't stop.

A few more before I wrap this up:

- ✔ Are you in need of afterschool care or caring for elderly parents? Try www.salvationarmyusa.org or www.catholiccharitiesusa. org.

- ✔ Are you in need of help with prescription medications? This is a killer expense for many people. Try www.helpingpatients.org.

- ✔ Are you a senior citizen in need of assistance with meals? Try www.fns.usda.gov/fdd/programs/nsip.

- ✔ Are you in need of meal assistance for your children at school? Try www.fns.usda.gov/cnd/lunch/.

- ✔ For funds for senior citizens to buy at local farmers markets, try www.fns.usda.gov/wic/SeniorFMNP/SFMNPmenu.htm.

- ✔ Are you a first time home buyer? Try www.hud.gov/offices/ or www.hud.gov/offices/cpd/affordablehousing/programs/home/ addi/.

- ✔ Are you buying a home in a rural area? Try www.rurdev.usda. gov.

- ✔ Are you a senior citizen wanting to learn about a reverse mortgage on your house, where it pays you every month? Try www.ftc.gov.

- ✔ Are you a college student? Try www.ed.gov/about/offices/list/ fsa/index.htm or www.studentaid.ed.gov.

✔ Are you wanting to continue on with your education? Try www.aauw.org/fga/fellowships_grants/.

✔ Are you wanting to learn a foreign language? Try www.ed.gov/about/offices/list/ope/iegps/index.html.

Stay current

As always, keep in mind that some of this website information may be fleeting, but I doubt it. These sites were accurate as of press time and most are agencies that will continue to be around for a long time. Changes in actual grant amounts or qualifications may occur every year. Agencies are constantly amending their programs, so do the research. You'll see what is out there right now and I bet you will find something that sparks your interest.

> The web is the best source for quick and easy access to all this free money.

If you do not have the internet at your house, go to your local library. The web is the best source for quick and easy access to all this free money. The print books on grants are cumbersome and can become obsolete. The internet is your new best friend.

For the directory of federal government agencies, you can visit www.firstgov.gov or www.pueblo.gsa.gov/call or 1-880-FED-INFO.

Detailed grant information is printed in hard copy in the Catalog of Federal Domestic Assistance and is available for $75. You can order it from the US Government Bookstore at bookstore.gpo.gov/actions/GeneralSearch.do. Let me warn you, this book is 2,400 pages!

Research project

Now you know why I suggest doing your research online and letting the search engines do the time consuming tasks for you. I opened this chapter stating the area of grants and programs is unbelievable. I bet you agree with me.

There are umpteen more programs I would love to tell you about, but you need to skim and scan and enter your information to see what works for you. Odds are, something will!

And don't forget to get the monthly newsletter to keep you informed of new information as it becomes available!

CHAPTER 24

More Breaking News

"It was the best of times, it was the worst of times."
~Charles Dickens

I can pontificate (I love that word) until the cows come home, and pontificate I have. I make a living by sounding off, and they—the government, the banks, the entire consumer lending industry—give me plenty to sound off about.

I have for years preached about the evils of their ways and now maybe we are seeing a slight change in the breeze of this administration as they pass new regulations. But the credit card companies just keep coming up with stuff that makes me scratch my head.

Things that make you go hmm ...

Here's the deal. The credit card companies and the banks put the screws to the American people and ripped us all off and then it came back to bite them on the butt. The economy tanked (partly in response to the wicked ways of these idiots) and they refuse to take any responsibility or do what they can to ease the stress.

Let's say you are a credit card holder of Advanta. They are hitting rough times (violin music please), so what do they do? They stick it to the cardholders.

Real nice.

Advanta is revoking the charge privileges of millions of customers. They specialize in cards for small business owners. Yes, that's right, the heartbeat of America. The hard-working citizens who make this country a better place.

Advanta is facing a cash crunch (crank the volume on that violin music). So what do they do? Nearly one million accounts get frozen. So small business owners who are also hitting the rough waters of this economy are left in the lurch with no credit card.

Huh?

Screwed up

It is the perfect case of We Screwed Up and It Hurt You and It Hurt Us Too; So to Make It Better We are Going to Hurt You More. Customer service? I don't think so.

This move was dubbed "unprecedented." No kidding.

In 2008, Advanta had a first quarter profit of $18 million. Obviously they are not too good at managing their money either. They laid off workers, cut dividends, and now they are cutting off their customers.

They hope that their customers will pay off their account balances, but the super folks at Advanta did not give their customers the courtesy of telling them that they were pulling the rug out from under them.

The report from the *Philadelphia Enquirer* states that customers were not notified: "Advanta customers contacted this week said the company still had not notified them of the cutoff."

"I was just on the phone with one of their representatives last week discussing payments, and they didn't even mention this," one customer stated, referring to the account closures. "It's ridiculous."

Business as usual

Advanta said in the Securities and Exchange Commission filing that it would contact customers "in accordance with applicable requirements." The company did not respond to a request for details.

Surprise, surprise.

In recent months, Advanta had jacked up the interest rates on their small business customers from single digits into the 20s and even 30% interest figures. Ouch.

> We should not be at their mercy.

When the going gets tough, stick it to the little guy. That seems to be their motto. Maybe when we go to print, this credit card company will have gone under. Hopefully, none of their former clients will be in that same predicament.

It makes me crazy. We should not be at their mercy. They giveth, and they taketh away. And in between, they jack up the rate and take you for everything you got.

I am not making this stuff up. As always, what really happens out there in the world is crazier than we could conjure up on our own. If you want to read the source of this news, take a look at www. philly.com/inquirer/business/20090523_Advanta_moves_up_card-freeze_date.html.

Tough lady

I wonder how anyone can keep up with this stuff. The Credit Card Holder Bill of Rights was passed in 2008, but the times keep changing. New Yorker Nancy Maloney has spearheaded the campaign for credit card rights for card holders for years.

It is an uphill battle.

So I guess I can't say every politician in Washington has blinders on or is taking bribes. There seem to be a few championing the cause.

Maloney says that everyone has a credit card horror story and I think we all would agree. I wish the stories would stop, but there always seems to be a new version right around the next corner. But we will never give up the fight.

Because things do happen.

You may not remember, but back in the "olden days" of ATM machines, the banks could hit you up for a fee for using a machine not at your own bank and you were not warned. Now, thanks to legislation passed in 1999, the banks must ask if you want to proceed with your transaction.

Little things mean a lot

You can choose to pay the fee, sometimes three bucks or more, or you can go find a machine in your bank system or go to the grocery store or gas station and use your debit card. Don't give the banks these fees! That's my operating procedure anyway.

Can you imagine if you did that all the time? What could you do with an extra thirty bucks a week? That's $120 a month. That just may be a minimum payment on a credit card. It could be groceries or dinner out. It could be a lot of things. So pay attention and do not just give your money away to the banks for the "convenience" of using their ATM machine.

And to get back on point, this one small change in ATM pro-cedures shows that writing your Congressmen and -women does make a difference. Make your voice and opinions known to those in Washington who are supposed to be representing you.

We can bring about the needed changes. Oh yes, we can.

Write

If you want to be heard, call, email, and write your elected officials. Many people do not know who "their people" are or how to contact them. Let me help.

www.senate.gov
www.house.gov

Tell them what is on your mind. If you have a specific situation, inform them of your hardship. If you want to voice your support for credit card industry reform, do so. If you want to ask for legislation on a particular issue, do so.

You elected your senators and congressmen. They are supposed to be working for you. Let them know what you want.

This just in

I don't want to end on a bitter note, but it would be appropriate since the whole point of this book is to point out the atrocities all around us.

However, I also like to share the information that makes your life better.

It also stresses the point that new information is popping up all the time. We are trying to get this book out of here and yet I keep learning new stuff that I need to share with you. That is why you need the monthly Debt Cures newsletter. So I can stay in touch and give you all the breaking news as it occurs.

Like this ...

In the Free Money sections, I told you about the $8,000 tax credit for first time homebuyers. It's a great deal and it just got better.

With a tax credit, you get the money when you file your tax return. Folks who qualify for this credit will buy the house in 2009. The 2009 tax return gets filed in early 2010 and that is when the credit money is received.

Usually.

> HUD spokesman stated it was a "real win for everyone."

As we go to print, the U.S. Department of Housing and Urban Development (HUD) announced that first time home-buyers using FHA-approved lenders can now get an advance on this $8,000 tax credit created by the stimulus package and apply it toward their down payments or closing costs.

Wow.

That is amazing. And wonderful.

Good news

In the report issued by CNN, (you can read it all for yourself online at money.cnn.com/2009/05/29/real_estate/tax_credit_as_downpayment/index.htm), the HUD spokesman stated it was a "real win for everyone." I concur.

He went on to say: "Families will now be able to apply their anticipated tax credit toward their home purchase right away. What we're doing today will not only help these families to purchase their first home but will present an enormous benefit for communities struggling to deal with an oversupply of housing."

Some states had already figured out that the tax credit was a great idea but the people wanting to buy a home needed the money up front for a down payment. These states created bridge loans to allow the home buyer to borrow against their coming credit and then be able to pay it back at tax time when they got their refund.

I love when common sense prevails.

The new deal offered now by HUD really does indicate that there is indeed hope for homeowners.

CHAPTER 25

Final Cures

"Success is how high you bounce when you hit bottom."
~ George Smith Patton

So much to say, so few pages.

I hope you feel armed and dangerous now, or at least confident to tackle your debt and move on. Getting on with your life is freedom.

Financial freedom opens doors.

Make the plays

Think of this book as a guidebook, a playbook. Using the tips, techniques, methods, and plays included here, you can increase your credit score. Maybe 100 points. Maybe 200, 300, or even 400 points.

Upping that credit score gives your life a whole new perspective. When your financial world falls right, it makes everything in your life seem better. Less stress can mean better health, better relationships, a better outlook.

You can take your credit card payments and cut them in half. Make those phone calls. Get rid of some of that debt. If it's old debt, you can eliminate it quite possibly in full! Remember all those magic words we discussed.

- ✔ Statute of limitations
- ✔ Alleged debt
- ✔ Identity Theft
- ✔ I demand …
- ✔ Would you …

My mom always told me to say please and thank you. I am telling you that there are more magic words that can open doors and create a new financial reality.

I want you to never feel the pressure of bill collectors ever again. You do NOT have to take their crap. They are not the golden court of truth, believe me.

The results of all these various debt cures methods and magic words are astounding. My friend had $15,000 wiped away when he realized the culprit, identity theft. I know people who had tens of thousands of dollars of debt wiped away when they realized it was old debt and it could not be collected. Take a look at the Appendix and you will see that it does not take long for debt to be deemed old debt.

Watch your language and you can save thousands and thousands of dollars. Words are powerful. Money talks. And sometimes silence speaks louder. Never admit that a debt may be yours. Many times the debt collectors know that it is not your debt or that it is old debt and they come after you anyway. Keep quiet and like a bad headache, the debt and the debt collector can disappear.

So many solutions

Things have gotten crazy in our economy, no doubt about it. Maybe you are having trouble with the house payment. You can apply some of these techniques and get your home mortgage renegotiated.

Maybe you just want to pay it off sooner. Done. You can do that without changing your monthly outlay. You can make money off of foreclosures and you can make money even if your own home is in foreclosure.

No matter how broke you are, there is always a way to make fast cash. Some of these ways can become a business, too, if that is your desire.

Too many people are paying too much in taxes. Pay attention to what tax credits you are entitled to and make sure you claim them. It is money in your pocket!

We shall be free ...

Take any one of these ideas in this book and apply it to your situation. I know these methods work. I know that you have the potential to save thousands of dollars.

> I know that you have the potential to save thousands of dollars.

I get cards and letters that prove it. The government and the credit card companies certainly don't like me. I call them on the carpet, actually, and expose them and what they do and how they rip off the American citizen. The truth always comes out.

Maybe in this new *Debt Cures 2* edition I was a kinder, gentler Kevin Trudeau. Maybe not. I am not backing down from my crusade to bring you the information and the knowledge and the power to fight back.

Our economy took a nosedive and we are not the ones to be blamed. We are the ones who are forced to pick up the pieces and move forward in our lives. I want to help all of you do that. I want to give assistance and offer ways to cure your debt problems. I want you to be debt free.

I want you to make your living doing what works for you. I don't want you bound by the chains of debt. Life is meant to be enjoyed.

When you apply one of these techniques and it works, you will be delighted, especially the skeptics who are reading. Then you will be emboldened to try another. And another. Then who knows, you might be among the throngs who write a testimonial to me.

Regular updates

Your letters and debt cures can get printed in the monthly newsletter. I encourage you to sign up. A book is too large a project to tackle to keep you constantly updated, but the newsletter is a wonderful tool to share breaking news in the industry and what methods are working for people just like you.

Curing your debt is the mission. Do you want to join this mission?

They—the banks, the credit card companies, the federal government—don't want you to know what is going on. They would prefer that you stayed in the dark and kept paying all their obnoxious fees.

I know the reality and now you do too. I also know that you do not have to stay down and out. You don't have to be their victim of highway robbery. You can defend yourself. And there need not be any bloodshed.

Just money. Your money. More of it for you, less of it for them.

Thanks for reading.

Kevin Trudeau

Sneak Peek

I also have another new book that I am very excited about. We called it *Kevin Trudeau's Free Money They Don't Want You to Know About.*

It is a complete book on FREE MONEY. This topic has become my passion. When we did the first *Debt Cures* book, I started to learn about all the free funding that is available. Government grants from state, local, and federal agencies. Private foundations offer money. Corporations have programs where they give free money.

Most people think you have to be poor or part of some sort of demographic to qualify. Nope.

There are grants for everyone and free money from other sources too. That is why this book is so much fun.

It's not just grants. It's sources that you would never think of and finding out is as easy as going online and typing in your name. It's like a great big party of lost and found money.

Free sample

I have millionaire friends who were able to use the tips in the *Free Money* book and they found money that they were entitled to.

Free money that you don't have to repay. It's better than the holidays.

I know I am little exuberant about this new project, but indulge me. I have included just a few pages for you. Imagine a whole book of ideas and sources of Free Money. I tell you where to find it. Names, addresses, phone numbers, websites. I tell you if you have to fill out an application or if it's just a name and social security number kind of thing.

Because I am so proud of this book, here is a tiny teaser taste for you.

Do you ever read fiction books and at the end, the author gives the first chapter of his or her new book to whet your appetite? I love that.

I grabbed a couple pages here for you. There is so much more. SO MUCH MORE!

Sneak peek

There are many private foundations that give free money as well. Want a sample?

Here you go.

Here are just some of the foundations that give personal and business grants:

- ✔ Wheless Foundation, P.O. Box 1119, Shreveport, LA 71152

- ✔ Simon & Schwab Foundation, P.O. Box 1014, Columbus, GA 31902

- ✔ Coulter Foundation, P.O. Box 5247, Denver, CO 80217

- ✔ Thatcher Foundation, P.O. Box 1401, Pueblo, CO 81002

- ✔ Biddle Foundation, Inc., 61 Broadway, Room 2912, New York, NY 10006

- ✔ Avery-Fuller Children Center, 251 Kearney Street, No. 301, San Francisco, CA 94108

✔ Jane Nugent Cochems Trust, c/o Colorado National Bank of Denver, P.O. Box 5168, Denver, CO 80217

✔ Unocal Foundation, P.O. Box 7600, Los Angeles, CA 90051

✔ Wal-Mart Foundation, 702 Southwest 8th Street, Bentonville, AK 72716

✔ The Piton Foundation, 511 16th Street, Suite 700, Denver, CO 80202

✔ Frank R. Seaver Trust, 714 W. Olympic Boulevard, Los Angeles, CA 90015

✔ Earl B Gilmore Foundation, 160 S. Fairfax Avenue, Los Angeles, CA 90036

✔ The Commonwealth Fund, One East 75th Street, New York, NY 10021-2692

✔ The Cullen Foundation, P.O. Box 1600, Houston, TX 77251

✔ The James Irvine Foundation, One Market Plaza, San Francisco, CA 94105

✔ William Penn Foundation, 1630 Locust Street, Philadelphia, PA 19103

✔ Blanchard Foundation, c/o Boston Sake, One Boston Place, Boston, MA 02106

✔ Xerox Foundation, P.O. Box 1600, Stamford, CT 06904

✔ Fairchild Industries, 20301 Century Boulevard, Germantown, MD 20874

✔ Charles and Els Bendheim Foundation, One Parker Plaza, Fort Lee, NJ 07024

✔ Blue Horizon Health & Welfare Trust, c/o Reid & Reige, Lakeville, CT 06039

✔ Broadcasters Foundation, Inc., 320 West 57th Street, New York, NY 10019

✔ Copley Fund, P.O.Box 696, Morrisville, VT 05661

✔ The Hawaii Foundation, 111 South King Street, P.O. Box 3170, Honolulu, HI 96802

✔ Inland Steel-Ryerson Foundation, 30 West Monroe Street, Chicago, IL 60603

✔ Northern Indiana Giving Program, 5265 Hohman Avenue, Hammond, IN 46320

✔ Cambridge Foundation, 99 Bishop Allan Drive, Cambridge, MA 02139

✔ Barker Foundation, P.O. Box 328, Nashua, NH 03301

✔ Morris Joseloff Foundation, Inc., 125 La Salee RD, W. Hartford, CT 06107

✔ Deposit Guaranty Foundation, P.O. Box 1200, Jackson, MS 39201

✔ Haskin Foundation, 200 E. Broadway, Louisville, KY 40202

✔ The Dayton Foundation, 1395 Winters Bank Tower, Dayton, OH 45423

✔ Ford Motor Company, The American Road, Dearborn, MI 48121

✔ Bohen Foundation, 1716 Locust Street, Des Moines, IA 50303

✔ Yonkers Charitable Trust, 701 Walnut Street, Des Moines, IA 50306

✔ Miles Foundation, P.O. Box 40, Elkhart, IN 46515

✔ Ametek Foundation, 410 Park Avenue, New York, NY 10022

✔ Horace B. Packer Foundation, 61 Main Street, Wellsboro, PA 16901

✔ John B. Lynch Scholarship Fund, P.O. Box 4248, Wilmington, DE 19807

✔ Camden Home for Senior Citizens, 66 Washington Street, Camden, ME 04843

✔ The Clark Foundation, 30 Wall Street, New York, NY 10005

✔ Richard & Helen DeVos Foundation, 7154 Windy Hill, SE, Grand Rapids, MI 49506

✔ Muskegon County Foundation, Fraunthal Center, Suite 304, 407 W. Western Avenue, Muskegon, MI 49440

✔ The H&R Block Foundation, 4410 Main Street, Kansas City, MO 64111

✔ New Hampshire Fund, One South Street, P.O.Box 1335, Concord, NH 03302-1335

✔ The Shearwater Foundation, Inc., c/o Alexander Nixon, 423 West 43rd Street, New York, NY 10036

✔ These foundations give grants for medical and education help:

✔ The Fasken Foundation, 500 West Texas Avenue, Suite 1160, Midland, TX, 79701

✔ The Rosario Foundation, 100 Broadway Avenue, Carnegie, PA 15106-2421

✔ Orange Memorial Hospital Corporation, P.O.Box 396, Orange, TX 77630

✔ The Perpetual Benevolent Fund, c/o Bay Bank Middlesex, 300 Washington St., Newton, MA, 02158, Attn: Mrs. Kelly.

✔ The Bagby Foundation for Musical Arts, 501 5th Ave., New York, NY 10017

✔ Larabee Fund Association, c/o Connecticut National Bank, 777 Main St., Hartford, CT 06115

✔ Battistone Foundation, PO Box 3858, Santa Barbara, CA 93103

✔ Avery-Fuller Children Center, 251 Kearney St., San Francisco, CA 94108

✔ Vero Beach Foundation for the Elderly, c/o First National Bank, 255 S. County Road, Palm Bch, FL 33480

✔ Smock Foundation, c/o Lincoln National Bank and Trust Co., PO Box 960, Fort Wayne, IN 46801

✔ Glifilin Memorial, Inc., W-555 First National Bank Building, St. Paul, MN, 55101

✔ Clarke Testamentary Trust/Fund Foundation, US National Bank of Oregon, PO Box 3168, Portland, OR, 97208

✔ Welsh Trust, PO Box 244, Walla Walla, WA 99362

Psst …

I can't stop myself. Free Money is everywhere …

How about free coupons?

Try:

✔ fatwallet.com
✔ couponchief.com
✔ coolsavings.com
✔ Pricegrabber.com
✔ smartaboutmoney.org

TO ORDER *KEVIN TRUDEAU'S FREE MONEY THEY DON'T WANT YOU TO KNOW ABOUT*, CALL 888-856-9046

Appendix

This statute of limitations information is correct to the best of my knowledge as we go to print. Be sure to check with an attorney or a friend or someone else in your state that is knowledgeable in these areas, in case the number of years for expiry of your debt has changed, and for any other relevant information.

STATE	OPEN ACCOUNTS (e.g., credit cards)	WRITTEN CONTRACTS
Alabama	3	6
Alaska	6	6
Arizona	3	6
Arkansas	3	5
California	4	4
Colorado	6	6
Connecticut	6	6
Delaware	3	3
Wash, DC	3	3
Florida	4	5
Georgia	4	6
Hawaii	6	6
Idaho	4	5
Illinois	5	10
Indiana	6	10
Iowa	5	10
Kansas	3	5
Kentucky	5	15

STATE	OPEN ACCOUNTS (e.g., credit cards)	WRITTEN CONTRACTS
Louisiana	3	10
Maine	6	6
Maryland	3	3
Massachusetts	6	6
Michigan	6	6
Minnesota	6	6
Mississippi	3	3
Missouri	5	10
Montana	5	8
Nebraska	4	5
Nevada	4	6
New Hampshire	3	3
New Jersey	6	6
New Mexico	4	6
New York	6	6
North Carolina	3	3
North Dakota	6	6
Ohio	4	15
Oklahoma	3	5
Oregon	6	6
Pennsylvania	4	4
Rhode Island	10	15
South Carolina	3	10
South Dakota	6	6
Tennessee	6	6
Texas	4	4
Utah	4	6
Vermont	6	6
Virginia	3	5
Washington	3	6
West Virginia	5	10
Wisconsin	6	6
Wyoming	8	10